THE ASQUINN TWINS
BOOK TWO

WHERE THE TRAIL FORKS

GRACE BROOKS

The Asquinn Twins Book 2: Where The Trail Forks
Revised edition

Copyright © Heather Radford
March, 2013

Published By Parables
October, 2016

All Rights Reserved. No part of this book may be reproduced or utilized in any form or by any means, electronic or mechanical, including photocopying, recording, or by any information storage and retrieval system, without permission in writing from the author.

Unless otherwise specified Scripture quotations are taken from the authorized version of the King James Bible.

First Edition   March, 2006
Revised Edition October, 2016

ISBN 978-1-945698-05-7

Printed in the United States of America

Readers should be aware that Internet Web sites offered as citations and/or sources for further information may have been changed or disappeared between the time this was written and when it is read.

The Asquinn Twins
Book Two
Where The Trail Forks

Grace Brooks

PUBLISHED by PARABLES
Earthly Stories with a Heavenly Meaning

Dedication

The Asquinn Twins and Where the Trail Forks is a work of fiction, which means all the characters are conjured out of my imagination and there are no real-life counterparts. The James Bay Frontier or Temiskaming District areas in the northern portion of the province of Ontario, Canada are the setting for this story and the series. Although I have used the right names for most of the towns, cities and rivers, I used a fictitious name for the town in my story.

The idea for the series did spring from an incident including the Ontario Provincial Police, Mom, and me that nipped my life of crime in the bud. For this I will forever be grateful and hold a deep respect for them which has spanned the years even though I do not live in Ontario anymore. All I will say about that incident is that one of the occurrences in the series almost duplicates my brush with the law, but I will not say which one.

Along with my gratitude, I say Ontario should be grateful they have the Ontario Provincial Police, and it's to this police force I dedicate the entire series.

Chapter One
Martha and Charlotte

Forest Lake, 1958

Martha stood by the row of horses, her face furious. She touched her companion's shoulder to get her attention. She wore auburn hair in a bun held in place with a at the back of her head.

"Sherry, look."

"What, Martha?"

Sherry looked in the direction in which sixteen-year-old Martha Asquinn pointed and caught sight of the vehicle on the gravel road, a cloud of dust billowing behind.

Sherry said, "That can't be more riders."

Martha breathed deeply as she walked down the row of tethered horses, filling each horse's container with oats and feeding them a handful of hay. She loved the smell of horses—hay, oats, the hay fields, the woods, leather and, yes, manure. But after her long day, mostly on her feet, her brand new western riding boots hurt her toes.

Each of the trail ride horses stood saddled, ready to be ridden, and tethered to hitching rails in a double row. One horse stood out in the midst of the line-up. A beautiful light taffy-coloured mare with black tail, mane and four black stockings to her knees.

Martha stopped by the mare. "Hello Taffy, you beautiful animal." Martha tweaked the mare's ears. Her brown eyes reflected the affection she held for the animal. Taffy whinnied her appreciation. Both girls laughed.

Martha looked up and all around her. Sherry paused brushing the mare, and rested a hand on the animal's back. With the other, she pushed her honey-coloured bangs away from her eyes. The rest of her thick, glistening, golden hair which she usually wore free and tumbling down to her waist, she had tied back in a ponytail.

"Yes, it is, and quitting time. The animals deserve a rest. It's been a busy day. So many trail riders, today." She rubbed a sweaty palm on one leg of her blue jeans.

Sherry held a handful of sweet hay under the mare's nose, which the horse eagerly gulped down with a snort of appreciation, then continued the brushing. She didn't stop again until she had run the brush down all four legs, and then went over the animal again, looking for sore spots.

Martha loved how her friend was so careful about checking for these tender spots and extra raw fly bites. She watched as Sherry then applied ointment to the horse's belly and under parts where the horseflies and mosquitoes bothered the most.

"Maybe this will stop the flies from tormenting you," Sherry said. "Once it's closer to sunset and the breeze has died down, the flies and mosquitoes are terrible."

Martha stroked the mare behind her ears and along her neck and body as Sherry began brushing out the mare's flowing mane and tail.

Eventually, Sherry set aside the brush and held another handful of hay beneath Taffy's muzzle.

Turning from the happy mare, the girls noticed that the car was closer.

Martha shook her head. She could see now that it was a polished, black Chevrolet Impala convertible, with the top down.

"It's only my wild brother driving like he owns the road."

They both watched as the car sped along the dusty, gravel trail and entered the stable yard. Ken stopped the car in a cloud of dust beside a storage building next to the horse-hitching rail. The horses whinnied low and danced about some, but that was it.

Nineteen-year-old Ken opened the driver's side door and stepped out. His friend, Bradan Turehue, did the same with the passenger side door, their shoes crunching on the gravel. Martin, who was in the back, also got out of the car and stood beside Martha, his twin.

Martha cringed as the two older boys slammed the doors too hard and shouted back and forth. Martin seemed the only responsible and steady one of the three.

An older man appeared in the doorway of the house across road separating the house from the stable. He strode down the steps and the short driveway to the road, which he crossed entered the stable yard. He stopped by the group. His hair was grey, but he stood straight.

"Mr. Greene, Forest Lake's eccentric resident," Martin said, meaning no disrespect.

"You guys, stop making so much noise around the horses. You'll spook them. I don't like you making so much noise around the livestock. I've warned you guys several times about it," he said.

Bradan wore baggy brown pants, a wide, brown leather belt and short-sleeved maroon shirt with black stripes down the front. He wore his hair cut short and neat. Martha watched with a sad heart, as he walked somewhat unsteadily towards her

Bradan walked up to Martha and glanced menacingly at Martin. Reluctantly Martin stepped away and went back to leaning against his brother's car.

Bradan took Martha in his arms and kissed her. She opened her arms to him. Her knees turned to butter as his brown eyes gazed into hers. She smiled at him. She ran her fingers through his short soft dark brown hair, much the same colour as her own. Bradan pushed the bangs aside and out of her brown eyes.

"And how are you, my Precious One?"

Martha loved it when he called her names like 'Precious one'. She fingered the beautiful engagement ring on her finger, where Bradan had placed it six years ago. Even if she'd wanted to rebuke him any further for the noise, her mouth went dry.

"I'm fine," she answered.

Martin stood to one side, arms crossed and toe tapping impatiently on the ground; not even trying to hide his annoyance with Bradan and Martha.

Ken walked up to Sherry, opened his arms wide, took her in his arms and kissed her. He also wore brown baggy pants, a wide black leather belt, and a tan shirt; his hair cut short and neat. His blue eyes looked into her hazel ones and in an instant, Sherry couldn't stand.

"How are you?"

Sherry couldn't answer for a moment. Ken had always affected her like that. She trembled whenever he entered the room or they stood together. He'd given her an engagement ring the same time as Bradan gave Martha hers.

"Fine." Sherry answered when she was able to talk.

Bradan realized Mr. Greene was still standing there watching them. "Ah, phooey on you old man. Take a look: Your hair is totally gray."

Martha's heart sank and a feeling of foreboding washed over her.

Ken waved a hand as if shooing away irritating deerflies.

"He may be an old man, but his frame is as straight and slim as a sapling, and his step is steadier that yours at the moment," Martha said with a snicker.

Bradan glanced at her. His brown eyes snapped anger. Martha fell silent knowing he wasn't happy that she commented on his condition. Martha turned to Sherry.

Ken left one arm around Sherry's waist as he added with a slur, "How long have you lived in Forest Lake, Mr. Greene? Since before the earliest white settlers?"

Martha knew her face was red with embarrassment.

She said, ashamed, "Ken don't be so unkind. And please lower your voice." Martha glanced nervously Mr. Greene's way. The old man stood at the railing, staring at her — at all four of them. Eventually, he left his spot near the hitching railing and entered the barn.

"Sherry, do you want to take orders from him all your life?" Ken asked.

Sherry brushed imaginary dust from her long sleeved western shirt. "Of course not, dearest Ken. This is only a summer job."

"Isn't it time for you to get off work?" Bradan asked.

"We don't quit until it's dark, Bradan dearest," Martha said.

"And you just couldn't get away early?" Ken said.

"Maybe," Martha said. "We don't seem at all busy this evening."

Mr. Greene appeared in the doorway of the stable, again, his words carrying remarkably strong and clear. "Girls, we have two people coming for a ride shortly. Be prepared when they get here."

"We will, Mr. Greene," Martha said. She glanced somewhat apprehensively at Sherry. Martha sighed when Mr. Greene went back inside the stable, then looked up at Bradan.

Sherry wriggled trying to get free of Ken, but his arm remained firm around her waist.

"We have to prepare a couple horses for the riders that are coming."

"They will be here any minute," Martha added.

Ken released Sherry. It was so sudden Sherry teetered on her feet, and almost fell.

"The horse that's the talk of the district. What's his name, Sunshine?"

"Taffy. And it's a she."

The mare flicked her ears at the mention of her name.

Ken moved closer to the mare with Martin right behind him. Martin's eyes swept over the animal.

"She isn't as large as most horses, but she is rather intelligent looking."

Mr. Greene hurried from the barn to join the group of young people.

"She's more than what most casual riders in this area can handle," he commented.

"Why?" Ken asked.

"She's of Arabian descent. That's why she's so spirited," Mr. Greene explained.

Ken scoffed at this.

Martin clasped Taffy's muzzle in his hands, pulled her head close to him and looked deeply into her eyes. "What a wonderful disposition!"

"That she is," Martha agreed. "Trouble is, most people can't even get into the saddle to ride her."

"She doesn't look very fierce," Bradan said.

"She's standing in the shade of the barn, lazily swaying back and forth as she sleeps," Ken scoffed.

Bradan stopped by Martha's side after circling the mare. "Her head is drooping over the railing. No one will convince me that this horse leaves more riders lying on the ground than those that rode her."

"Just try getting on the saddle," Martha said.

Ken snapped his fingers loudly. "I have an idea, Bradan. Let's you and I go for a ride."

Bradan held up his hands. "No way."

"Aw, come on."

"This ought to be fun. And what horse do you intend to use?" Martha asked.

"I'll use Taffy. Bradan will want a horse like that palomino there that's so old he can barely move beyond a trot."

"You can count me out."

"All right, I will go on my own." He turned to his brother. "I have a better idea, Martin will go with me."

"You won't go on your own," Martha said. "It's against the rules. You can wait until the other two riders arrive and we'll all go out together."

Ken waved these ideas away. "Rules? I'm not ten years old. I can look after myself."

"One of us has to go with the riders each trip," Martha insisted.

Ken said patiently, "Martha, my horse, please."

Martin stepped in before his twin could answer. "Not in your condition."

"There's nothing wrong with my condition. My horse!"

Martha worked the bit into Taffy's mouth and tightened the bridle. Sherry tightened the belly cinch. Taffy laid her ears back at this attention.

"Oh no. Going out again?" Martha said sympathetically to the horse. Martha untied the rope from the hitching rail and led the horse to stand by Ken. The horse appeared to be half asleep, her eyes closed and ears resting.

Martha held the reins and stood by the mare's head to keep the animal calm while Ken tried to get into the saddle.

Taffy remained docile-looking enough until Ken had one foot in a stirrup and was swinging himself up into the saddle, then she exploded and started to buck. Before Ken could get a foothold, he found himself in a heap on the ground. Most riders took the first fall seriously, but Taffy's actions had riled the alcohol in Ken's blood.

"Give me those reins."

Martha handed him the leather straps. She stopped breathing as her brother swung them over the mare's head and onto her neck. Holding the reins tight, Ken lifted the usual foot first into a stirrup then swung upwards and into the saddle. He chuckled as he swiftly found the second stirrup. Martha started breathing again.

"There, you stupid horse, I got the better of you didn't I?"

But Taffy wouldn't admit it and started bucking again.

Ken held on for a while then, like so many other riders, he lost his grip on the saddle and landed in a heap on the hard-packed ground. The wind whooshed out of him with a loud humph. All he could do was lie in one spot and wait until he could move again.

Taffy trotted back to the line of horses to her tie up spot, snorting and shaking her head.

Bradan rushed to his fair- headed friend.

"Are you all right?"

The girls tee-heed.

Ken groaned and stirred and drew a reluctant breath. "I'm all right."

Bradan helped him to his feet.

Ken had been riled before. Martha saw he was even more so now. She also

saw Mr. Greene standing in the barn door, so he had seen everything.

Chapter Two
Ill Luck for The Boys

A pair of broken reins waiting for repair hung from a nail on the outside of the barn door. Martha held her hand to her heart as Ken spied them, stalked up to the door and jerked one broken end from its perch.

"What are you doing?" Martha demanded.

"I'm going to teach that horse she can't dump me like that."

"Ken, don't," Martin said.

"You shouldn't have been riding her in the first place. Taffy's here for the more experienced riders," Martha added.

Ken favoured his brother and sister with a scathing look. "Since when was it your place to tell me what to do?"

"Since you are in no condition to make good judgments," Martin told him.

Ken ignored Martin and strode past the other horses to where Taffy stood. He raised the leather rein above his head, but before he could bring the leather strap down on the horse's rump, Mr. Greene stormed over and grabbed his hand. He snatched the rein from Ken's hand and flung it over a fence rail.

"What do you think you are doing?"

Martha's throat tightened, making it difficult to breathe.

"She bucked me off. Am I just supposed to let her get away with that?"

"There's better ways to calm a high-spirited horse than to whip it!"

Taffy had not been expecting this. She whinnied in terror and jumped forward, right through the hitching post railing. With reins and stirrups flapping, she galloped straight for the barn and the wide door on the side, and inside.

"Mr. Greene, I'll go calm her." Martha entered the barn and, with Martin following her, went into the mare's stall.

"There now," she said in a soothing tone, while running her hands over Taffy's back. Taffy snorted her agitation at first but, gradually, the horse calmed.

When she was satisfied that Taffy was alright, she and Martin went back outside where Mr. Greene was still confronting Ken.

"You are nothing but a drunken fool. I can smell it on your breath." Ken was beyond speech as Mr. Greene continued. "Look at you, drunk the way you are and you, the son of the minister; minister of a church that's supposed to be the pillar of Christianity."

He turned to Bradan.

"And you're a member of that church. If this is an example of what kind of people your church turns out no wonder so many people don't want anything to do with your religion. What kind of Christians are you?"

"They are back-slidden Christians," Martin said.

"And what does that mean?" Mr. Greene asked.

Sherry explained. "It means they're still Christians but, because they've lost fellowship with God, are poor examples of what a Christian should be."

"Baa," Mr. Greene exploded. "I don't want to hear that. You two, I want you two off this property, now."

Bradan said in an offended tone, "Come on, Ken. Let's cut out."

Bradan started back to Ken's car and Ken followed. Martin remained with the girls. As they reached the car, a brilliant red, top-down convertible, drove up and stopped. A young woman and a young man stepped out.

"Those are our trail riders," Mr. Greene said to Martha. "Make sure they get their money's worth."

Martha left the group and walked up to the newcomers. A young man in his late teens held out his hand to her. She grasped his hand and they shook.

"My name's Jim. This is Gloria."

"I'm Martha, and this is Sherry," Martha said. "This is my twin brother, Martin."

Ken swaggered up behind her and stopped by the new girl.

"My name is Ken Asquinn."

Martha could see that Jim was offended by Ken's boldness.

"Ken, behave," Martha begged.

"Don't pay any attention to him, Gloria. He's not even sober."

"How about going on a date with me tonight?" Ken continued.

"But I'm dating someone."

"Who? Him?" Ken responded without even glancing at Jim. Martha was shocked. Martin raised his eyebrows.

"Yes, him."

"Come out with me and I can show you a better time." Ken didn't seem to care who heard him.

"No, thank you."

Gloria turned away, moving towards her escort.

Martha glanced at Sherry.

"My brother, your fiancé, couldn't be flirting with this girl?" she said.

"So, he asked her for a date." Sherry tried to appear like she wasn't bothered by Ken's actions.

Martha was surprised at her friend's lack of concern about her fiancé's flirting. She glanced at Martin who merely shrugged and threw up his hands.

Sherry smiled. "Such exquisite features. He deserves the attention he gets from other females. I think he was just being funny."

Anger washed through Martha. Bradan was just as handsome as Ken. She knew Sherry would be offended if she didn't think her brother was good looking.

"Ken is your brother, my future husband. We both know him well enough to realize he likes to tease and if he can get people worked up and cross with him, so much the better. Gloria turned him down, so I have nothing to get distressed over."

Martha looked around her and sighed when she saw Mr. Greene

struggling to repair the broken hitching rail. He passed Ken and Bradan on one of his trips to gather the necessary tools and material.

"Are you two idiots still here? I thought I told you to get off this property and not come back. You disturb the horses."

"Damn." Ken turned to Sherry before he slid behind the wheel. "We'll be back to get you when you're done work."

"We'll be looking for you."

Jim and Gloria looked over the mounts.

Martha brought Taffy from her stall.

Gloria fell in love with the mare on first sight.

"That's the one I want to ride! What's her name?"

"Her name is Taffy," Martha answered, "and there are some things you ought to know about her."

After repeating what she'd just told Ken and Bradan, Martha handed Gloria the reins and said, "Climb aboard."

Martha stood beside the mare's head with the reins short in her hand, but Gloria would have none of it. She held the reins in her hand and vaulted into the saddle on her own, so swift and skillful it took both Martha and Taffy by surprise.

Gloria found both stirrups and her two feet grounded firm in a flash. Gloria raised the end of the reins high enough for the mare to see and said in a no-nonsense tone,

"Try some funny tricks if you dare." She waved the ends of the reins. Taffy behaved.

Martha looked at Mr. Greene, a smile softening his leathered, sun-browned face. "At last! Someone who knows how to handle that mare."

Ken waited until the wide spot in the shoulder of the road and pulled the car over. On their right, a field stretched away from them and the trail that took the riders and horses over these open fields was clearly visible from the road. This was a popular spot for motorists to stop and watch the riders pass by.

"Why did you stop here?" Martin asked from the back seat.

"I have an idea," Ken said.

Bradan glanced at his fair-haired friend from the passenger seat. "What are you going to do? You didn't park here simply to watch the riders go by. You were really angry when that mare dumped you and then Gloria did." Laughter burst from his mouth, but an angry glance from

Ken silenced him.

"Twice in one evening," Ken said scornfully. "I'm going to teach both of them a lesson."

"You're what?" Martin said, sickened with his brother's behaviour.

"I'll teach her she can't get away with refusing me a date, and Mr. Greene has to learn he can't talk to me the way he did. When they come along, I'm going to blow the car's horn. That ought to scare the horse enough to buck that stuffed shirt, Gloria, off."

"Ken, you are engaged to Bradan's sister," Martin said. "Why should you even think of asking another girl for a date, especially when the girl you are to marry was right there."

Ken didn't reply. Bradan remained silent and Ken looked his way. He sat with his head resting on the back of the seat.

"Can you blame me for wanting to get them back?" Ken said.

"No, I don't," Bradan said.

"Look," Martin said. "They're not far away, and my sister's in the lead."

Ken and Bradan looked across the field.

Bradan's face saddened. "She was my Martha."

"Now!" Ken cried and pressed the horn, emitting several ear-splitting blasts.

In the field nothing happened. The four horses remained calm with all four feet on the ground.

Ken scowled.

"Well, I guess that didn't work," Martin said, relieved. "Can we go now?"

"Not on your life," Ken snapped. "Perhaps they were still too far away."

The boys did not notice the truck just about to pass on the road beside them. Ken was about to blast the horn again when the truck rumbled by, and loose fishing tackle fell to the truck bed floor with a loud crash as they went over a bump.

In the field, At at first it seemed that nothing was happening, then suddenly Taffy whinnied, reared and flayed the air in front of her with her front legs.

Martin, Ken, and Bradan watched in horror as the mare stood suspended on her hind legs for what seemed like an awfully long time, then went over backward and fell, then rolled, on her rider.

This unnerved Bradan.

"Oh my goodness," Bradan gasped. "Floor it, Ken!"

"Good idea," Ken agreed. "And, Bradan, get rid of that cursed flask."

Ken fumbled with the keys in the ignition, and in a few seconds had the engine running.

With tires spraying gravel, Ken sped down the road. As they passed a wooded, swampy area, Bradan rolled down his window and launched the flask out the window.

Bradan sighed. "Sink out of sight forever, and never be recovered."

Not one of the three looked .

Ken drove straight home and parked his car in the family parking area and switched off the engine.

"Bradan, my friend, I'll see you tomorrow. I'm not feeling well. Have to get to bed and pile up some Zs."

Martin winced as Ken climbed out of his car and slammed the door. He hoped Ken wouldn't disturb the rest of the family.

Then Martin noticed Bradan sat slumped in his seat, passed out cold. Martin shook him, and Bradan woke up with a startled gasp and looked around him.

"Where am I? Are we still in your car, Ken? Or are we in mine? Am I home yet?"

"We're still in Ken's car. We just parked in front of our house. Come on, we both have to go home. Will you be alright?"

"I'm fine," Bradan said.

Martin took him at his word, closed the car door and hurried to catch his older brother.

It was darker now and objects outside mere shadows. Ken staggered along the driveway to the porch door. He caught up with Ken in time to see him try the knob and the door open so suddenly and unexpectedly that Ken stumbled forward.

Ken wobbled through the kitchen and fell as Martin arrived in the open doorway and exchanged frustrated looks with his mother.

When Ken looked up, his parents were looking right at him. He peeked into the living-room. The faces of four younger siblings looked back at him.

It grieved Martin to see the pain on his mother's beautiful face at the sight of her son, the child of her heart. Ken pushed himself to his feet and stood, leaning against the wall for support.

"Ken, I realize you didn't do this to intentionally aggravate the family, but couldn't you be quieter opening and closing the car doors?" Pastor Asquinn said.

"Not my fault the parking spot just happens to be right under yours and Mom's bedroom window," Ken said.

Pastor Asquinn reached out to offer his son help, but Ken shrugged his hands off. Pastor Asquinn reached to help him a second time.

With Martin on one side for support and Pastor Asquinn on the other and Mother following, they made their way down the hall to the end bedroom which Martin and Ken shared. With one foot, Ken slammed the door behind them.

"Try to be quiet," Pastor Asquinn said tenderly. "I'm almost certain you've made enough noise to disturb the neighbours."

The bed-springs groaned a protest as Ken dropped on the mattress.

At Mother's next glare, Martin knew what was coming.

"How about telling me what went on tonight?"

Dad glanced at Ken.

"Give me a break, and let me go to sleep," Ken said.

Ken waved at the bed opposite him and asked his brother, "Aren't you going to sleep?"

"You mean, put up with you and your snoring again? When you wake after a night like this you are worse than a Grizzly Bear. I think I'd rather sleep on the couch in the living-room."

Martin, Pastor Asquinn and Mrs. Asquinn left the room, closing the door gently behind them.

"Really, he is a good man," Mother said.

"I know," Martin agreed, heaving a sad sigh. Then his head jerked up and he looked from Mom to Dad. "We didn't go back to get Martha."

"Didn't she come with you?"

"They had a couple late riders come in and so we promised to go back and get them, and we didn't."

Mother gave an angry humpf, pivoted, then left the room.

Pastor Asquinn said to Martin, "Come on, you and I will go for Martha and Sherry."

Chapter Three
Alone

Martha tried to push Bradan and Ken's behavior from her mind, as she urged her horse to walk next to Taffy so she could be close enough to check the mare's behavior. But Gloria seemed to know what she was doing – and Taffy knew it too. When Gloria touched the mare's sides with her heels, Taffy meekly started walking along the trail that took them across an open field to woods beyond. Gloria pulled on the reins and the mare obediently slowed to walk alongside Martha. Jim and Sherry remained behind, Sherry a little ahead of Jim.

"You and your friend…what's her name?" Gloria asked.

"Charlotte. Sherry for short," Martha replied.

"I noticed you both are wearing engagement rings."

"That's right. To those two boys that were at the stables when you arrived."

"The four of you are so young. How old are you girls, fifteen?"

"Seventeen in the fall. You don't look so old yourself, Gloria."

Gloria blushed, but instead of responding to Martha, said, "And the boys?"

"Almost twenty. They will turn twenty shortly after they enter police academy in Regina."

Jim's eyes opened wide. "Regina? You mean they're training to be--?"

"That's right, Mounties," Martha said.

"How much more lucky could two girls get?" Gloria said. "Their profession is really some calling."

"I suppose so," Martha said, not really sure what that meant. "Our plans are to get married after they graduate and have a double ceremony police wedding."

"Wow," Gloria said. "Your lives are really mapped out for you. How lucky. So, which one is yours?"

"Bradan."

"Which one was he? Is he the tall and dark-haired one that asked me out?"

"No, that was Ken, my older brother. The one that looked like me is Martin, my twin. Bradan is the other one."

"Oh," Gloria said. "I noticed him."

They arrived at the field running parallel to the road. The riders paused, side by side for a moment. Martha looked upwards and noticed the sun just about even with the tree tops and the shadows from the trees lengthened and darkened. She glanced at her watch. Ten o'clock.

Across the field on the road she saw Ken's car parked in a favourite viewing spot curious people stopped to watch trail riders pass. Often, she and Sherry noticed people watching, so neither one thought it strange to see Ken's car. Martha also noticed a truck approaching from the opposite direction. A car horn sounded. The horses remained calm and steady as the group ventured farther into the field. Thinking the boys were saying hello, Martha and Sherry waved.

Then everything went crazy. As the truck passed Ken's parked car, it hit a bump and a loud, sharp sound echoed through the still evening as a tool box in the back of the truck hit the truck box bottom and broke open. Fishing lures spilled all over the truck box,r.

Taffy screamed, reared and flayed her front feet in the air. Mouth open wide, Sherry watched in horror as the mare went over backward and landed on her back, pinning her rider under the saddle. Jim's face drained of all colour as Gloria cried at the impact, then lay still and pale-white after Taffy rolled off. All three watched in unbelief as the mare flayed her four legs in the air, rolled and regained her feet. Gloria still lay pale and unmoving..

Then Martha came alive. Swiftly, she swung out of her saddle and ran to Gloria's side. She fell to her knees in the grass and checked her breathing. Jim and Sherry were also on the ground in a flash. Sherry paused to look around for Taffy but the horse had taken off, so she joined Jim and Martha kneeling by Gloria. Jim felt for her pulse.

"What made that noise?" Martha said.

"I don't know," Sherry said. "The noise came from the truck."

The girls looked at Jim for an answer.

"A tool box of some kind loose in the back of the truck got knocked over from the bump," Jim said. "I will go back and talk to Mr. Greene," Martha said, then mounted her horse again and kicked the mare into a gallop.

Mr. Greene had just closed and latched the gate to Taffy's outside corral when Martha stopped by the barn door.

"You need to call the police."

Mr. Greene's eyes widened. "What happened? Where are the rest?"

Martha told him the story. When she'd finished, Mr. Greene hurried across the road to his house to make the phone call. Martha jumped back on her horse and galloped back to the accident scene.

A few minutes later, Mr. Greene shuffled in on foot.

"The boys in blue are sending an officer or two, and an emergency vehicle from Lakeview."

When the ambulance arrived, Martha, Sherry, Jim, and Mr. Greene watched as Gloria was examined and readied for transport to the hospital, then as she was lifted onto a stretcher and into the back of an emergency van.

"She's still alive, isn't she?" Martha said.

"She's still breathing," one of the medics replied.

Before the van's doors closed behind Gloria, Jim tried hopping in the back of the ambulance, but one of the police officers put out an arm and stopped him.

"We have some questions for you to answer. You will be free to go once we're through with our questions."

The police started interviewing everyone, including neighbours who might have seen or heard something.

"You will have to destroy that mare, Taffy," one police officer told Mr. Greene. "I believe you were warned about this once before. She's an accident waiting to happen."

When he heard this, Mr. Greene was so distraught he looked like he wanted to tear out his hair. Martha felt sorry for her boss until he turned to Martha and her friend.

"It was those boyfriends of yours that spooked her, wasn't it? Those fools didn't even know what they were doing. I should have had them arrested; they were drunk and disorderly. Now, because of them I will have to get rid of a beautiful and intelligent mare."

Sherry jumped to her sweetheart's defence.

"Mr. Greene, I think it's unfair of you to accuse Ken of something terrible like this before you have all the facts."

"It wasn't them that caused all this," Martha backed up her friend.

"What else could it be? Those two spooked the horses the entire time they were here. I will likely have to give up my livelihood now."

"Why would you have to do that?" Martha said.

"It was only Taffy that had a reputation for being difficult," A police officer reminded him. "That shouldn't stop your customers from riding the other horses."

Mr. Greene's shoulders hunched, the first time Martha had seen him not standing up straight.

"Once an accident like this happens with one horse then customers tend to be nervous about any other horse in the string. I'm ruined. And it's all because of those loaded boys."

Mr. Greene gathered up the reins of girls' horses

"I know this wasn't your fault, girls, but I'm afraid I won't need your services any longer. I can finish up for the night."

"Mr. Greene, we have three witnesses saying there was no vehicle but the truck in the area when this all happened. I can't see how the boys in the car can be responsible."

"Baa!" Mr. Greene said and dismissed them with a wave.

Martha and Sherry watched Mr. Greene lead their horses into the barn. When the police said they didn't have anymore questions and drove away, the girls turned and started to walk back across the field.

Sherry looked at Martha. "What do we do now?"

"We can walk back towards the road," Martha said. "The boys should be waiting for us by now."

"I hope so. It will soon be dark," Sherry said.

The girls made their way across the uneven ditch, stumbled their way up onto the gravel road, through the lengthening shadows.

"I don't see Ken's car," Sherry said.

"Or Bradan's car," Martha said. "What now?"

"We sit and wait," Sherry said.

"Mr. Greene might let us use his phone to phone home for a ride?" Martha said.

"I don't ever want to go there again," Sherry said decisively. "He was very unfair in accusing our future husbands. It wasn't the car horn that scared her."

"I agree," Martha said.

The girls sat down on the edge of the road and waited. And waited. And waited with only the stars in the heavens for company. The night and darkness didn't wait.

"It's really quite a nice night," Martha said after a long moment of silence, her eyes on the stars above.

"Yeah, gorgeous enough to be sitting in the dark waiting for my sweetheart to come drive me home," Sherry grumbled. "It's damp and I am chilly."

The girls fell silent.

Ten minutes went by before Sherry broke the quiet. "Martha?"

"What?"

"Do you think Bradan and Ken have lost their Christian testimony?"

Martha nodded, though Sherry probably couldn't see it.

"It sure seems like it. I pray every day that God will bring my Ken back to the close fellowship with Jesus that he once enjoyed."

"And I do the same with Bradan."

"Do you still want to marry him?"

"What do you mean?"

"Bradan isn't as well behaved as they were when we were ten and thirteen. Ken thinks nothing about missing church. And, while I don't think their behavior spooked Taffy in hurting Gloria, they weren't exactly acting like good Christian young men."

"And Ken has said he would rather be out having..." Sherry made a curling motion in the air with her fingers "... 'fun' somewhere than come to midweek service."

"Bradan swears and takes God's name in vain, too, just as often and as easily as an unsaved person."

The friends fell silent again. Martha drew patterns in the sandy shoulder of the road with a stick. She realized she had drawn her love's face in the dust. Sherry sat and shivered and turned the expensive diamond ring on her finger around and around. Martha spoke first.

"Here are my thoughts on Bradan. God intended me to love Bradan. Whether he does good or bad. I don't believe I should criticize him. Instead of wishing my intended husband is the man he isn't, I'll love him the way he is."

"And I ought to continue to pray that God will turn Ken back to the strong and meaningful relationship he had with Him before."

Martha thought for a while. "Why don't we say prayers for those boys right here and now."

"Good idea."

Martha bowed her head, and Sherry followed.

"You go first," Sherry said.

"All right. Father in Heaven, I want to take this opportunity to pray for my beloved Bradan. I know he is not standing in your word as strongly as he used to, something else has caused him to stray. But you are stronger than anything that holds him in its grip, and can cause whatever holds him to go away and bring him back to you."

When Martha paused, Sherry continued. "And I want to ask the same for Ken. He does not have the same desire to stand for you as he once did. Please change this and bring him back to you in an even stronger relationship than he enjoyed before."

Both girls said, "Amen."

"I won't desert Bradan. I'm not giving up on him. He needs me more than he's willing to let on."

"That's the way I feel about Ken. I will marry him come what may. I loved him when I was ten years old and I love him now."

"And I love Bradan. Nothing is going to get in the way of me marrying him."

The girls fell silent as if their thoughts and words had drained them of their strength.

"But I do wish one would come for us and drive us home. How about Martin, Martha? Would he come for us if we phoned your place?"

"Probably, but I don't want to go back to Mr. Greene's house and the Jamesons over on East Ridge don't have a phone. The next phone is your house, or ours. Besides, Martin only has a beginner's driver's license."

Sherry sighed. "You're right."

A car's lights blazed through the night, blinding the girls.

Sherry said in a whisper, "Could that be Ken come for us at last?"

"Or maybe Bradan," Martha said.

The girls eagerly rose to their feet, but the car continued on by.

"Guess not," Martha said. "Let's walk. It's better than just sitting here. Plus, it'll keep us warm."

With only the stars to provide adequate light, Martha and Sherry stumbled along in the darkness, back towards town. The girls had just rounded the point of East Ridge when car lights approached ahead of them.

"Think it's them?"

Sherry shrugged, after the disappointment of the first car, she dared not get her hopes up that rescue was at hand.

"Let's keep walking," Martha said.

Someone in the passenger seat rolled down the window as the car came to a stop beside the girls. Martha continued walking, but Sherry hung back.

"But Martha, maybe we shouldn't refuse a ride. I'm cold and my feet are tired."

Sherry moved towards the car, but Martha grabbed her by one arm and dragged her away.

"No, Sherry. We mustn't," Martha hissed in her ear. "Thanks, guys."

"Refusing rides from boys is not the way to be popular," Sherry said.

"Don't worry about being popular. We're better off walking on our own."

"I don't know about that. It's so dark. Why is it so much darker on the ground by our feet than higher in the sky?"

"Ouch!" cried Sherry after a stone clattered away from her foot.

"You girls want a ride?"

"There's plenty of room in here," another voice piped up.

Never in her lifetime Martha felt so relieved to hear those voices. "Da! Martin!"

The driver's side door opened and Martin leaped out into the dark night and dashed around the car and held the back door open.

"Did you girls hear about the accident at Greene's riding stable?" Da asked once they were under way.

"What did you hear?" Sherry asked.

"A loco horse rolled over on his rider," Martin said.

"We know all about it," Martha said.

"The story goes that the young girl will never walk again," Da said.

Martha and Sherry looked at each other.

"Where did you here that?" Martha said.

"From the car radio news," Martin said. "The newscast was on only a few minutes ago.

The car approached the first house, Sherry's. Bradan's was parked in the driveway.

"Bradan's car is home," Martha said. The girls looked across the road to the wide expanse of the church parking lot next to Martha's home.

"So is Ken's," Sherry said. "But why he didn't come to drive me home?"

"Bradan must have a good reason," Martha said.

Martin and Pastor Asquinn exchanged smiles.

"I wouldn't say a good reason," Pastor Asquinn said.

"Anyway, I'm too tired to reason it all out. I'm going inside and to bed. But first I'll see you inside," Martha said.

Martha followed Sherry inside. The two of them dashed upstairs and paused at Sherry's doorway. Martha glanced down the hallway at Bradan's door. It was closed. On an impulse she went to his door and quietly opened it.

"Bradan." She called softly but there was no response. The bed covers were unruffled. Clearly, the bed had not been slept in. Puzzled, she turned and went back to Sherry who was in her own room preparing for bed.

"Nighty-night," Martha said.

"Good-night," Sherry called to her through the darkness.

Martha slowly closed the doors as she left the house. She passed Ken's car unaware that Bradan was sleeping in it.

Mother stood in the shadows in the hallway by the living-room door. She remained still as Martha, Martin and Da entered the kitchen and locked the doors. Martha was about to step into the small hallway from the kitchen to living-room to go to bed when she saw her mother.

"Er, hi."

"Where have you been?" Mother asked. "It is one o'clock in the morning."

"Sherry and I waited for Ken or Bradan to pick us up. When no one showed up, we decided to walk."

Martin stepped in and explained. "When we got home after we left you and Sherry, Ken went right to bed. Barely made it down the hall, actually. And Bradan passed out in Ken's car and apparently is still there."

Mother hugged her. "I'm just glad you're home safe. I was so worried. Heaven knows what could have happened to you even in this little town." She let her go.

Da said, "As it is, you will have some explaining to do in the morning."

"Well then, be angry with Ken. It was him that promised to be back to drive us home; and he didn't show up. It's not fair to be angry with me."

Martha yawned.

"Well, now maybe this household can get some sleep," Mother said.

Martha left her brother in the living room and headed down the hall to the room she shared with her little sister, Faith. She stripped down to her underwear, then climbed in under the covers and was asleep before her head touched the pillow.

Chapter Four
Lectured

The sun was high above the tree tops when Martha awoke. She dressed and walked into her brothers' room. She paused when she saw Martin, also fully dressed, sitting on the edge of his bed. She went to the window and drew back the curtains to let in the brilliant sunlight.

"We need sunlight in here..." She trailed off when she looked at Martin and caught him peering down at his brother with a sad look on his face. Ken lay still in his bed, dead to the world. Martha moved closer to her twin and laid a comforting hand on Martin's shoulder. "I'll help you pray for him."

The twins knelt by the side of Martin's bed and prayed.

Ken rolled over on his other side, facing into the room.

"Mom, did you just open those damn curtains?" He closed his eyes against the sharp pain.

"Mom didn't. I did," Martha said.

Ken groaned, then pushed himself to his elbows.

"Might as well get dressed. Excuse me, sister."

Martha left, shutting the door with a louder sound than she intended.

A muffled "Damn!" came from inside.

short time later, Ken entered the kitchen, Martin trailing after him. Here there were no curtains on the window and Martha felt deep sympathy for him when he closed his eyes against the pain caused by the bright light. He stopped so suddenly Martin bumped into him.

Ken glanced behind him at his younger brother.

"Why are you sticking so close to me?"

"Someone has to make sure you don't bang into something and break your fool neck."

Ken opened his mouth to answer, but changed his mind and continued to the kitchen table. Martha was already there, with their parents, eagerly devouring a plate of food. Ken pulled out a chair and sat down across from Martha. Martin sat beside his twin.

At the sight of food, Ken put a hand over his mouth.

"And how is my boy this morning?" Mother asked of Ken.

Martha giggled.

"How do you feel this morning?" their Da inquired.

"I'm fine." Even the act of sitting down in a chair caused waves of pain to shoot through his head. He was far from feeling fine.

"I would like some of that nice juice, please," Ken said, looking at Martha. "Will you please get me a glass of juice?"

"Sure." Martha got up, went to the refrigerator and took out a juice container. After pouring some in a glass, she set it in front of her older brother.

"Enjoy."

"Thank you, you are a dear sister." Ken took a sip.

"You are welcome," Martha said. Only the ticking of the kitchen clock could be heard in the following silence.

"Too bad you didn't think Sherry was dear enough last night to go back for and drive home after she was finished with work," Mother said.

"What are you talking about?" Ken set the emptied glass down on the table. "Another one, please."

Martha pointed at the juice container, indicating to her brother he was to fill his own glass.

"She didn't get home this morning until after midnight," Mother enlightened Ken. "Which means Sherry didn't either."

Ken had to swallow more juice before he could he could ask, "Why not?"

"Because you said you'd come back for us, so we waited and waited for you. Neither you nor Bradan showed up to drive us home," Martha answered.

"I was home early last night," Ken argued, vaguely remembering. "I must'a went to bed and slept."

"You were passed out, drunk," Da amended lightly. "There is quite a difference."

Ken's face turned white and Martha knew he was starting to remember.

"Dad and I had to help you to bed," Martin continued.

Ken swallowed more juice to wet his dry throat, and Martha knew what was coming. Da would lecture him until he felt like screaming.

Hoping to counteract the coming lecture, Ken said, "Sherry isn't making a federal case of this is she? Those girls could have found another ride home."

"They did, finally," Martin said. "Dad and I brought them home—after they started walking."

Ken scoffed at this. "There you go. Those girls would have a nicer time if they weren't so afraid a boy will violate them if one of them happens to smile at him or if he smiles at one of them."

"That's enough of that kind of talk," Da said, sternly.

Silence hung in the kitchen for a few moments until Da said, "You must have had a good time last night."

Ken merely blinked. "I don't remember. I'll have to ask Bradan when I see him."

"I want to know what you drank last night."

"I don't know. All I remember it had quite a kick to it. Vodka maybe. Bradan supplied the liquid."

Da shook his head sadly. "Oh, Ken. That stuff is strong. You don't feel the effects right away. They come later."

"It sure did. We had the best night of our lives."

"Ken, I don't like you talking this way," Mother said.

"I can talk anyway I like. I am almost twenty. I'm an adult now."

"That may be, but you still live under my roof and as long as you do, you will live by the house rules. And that includes no drinking," Da said, then added as Ken lit a cigarette, took a deep drag, then blew a cloud of blue smoke into the air, "or smoking. Put that foul weed out."

"Oh, for Pete's sake. Dad, you are overbearing." He kept on smoking.

Martin patted Mother on the back as she reached across the table and pulled the package of cigarettes from Ken's shirt pocket and threw it into the garbage can beside the refrigerator.

"There will be no more smoking in this house, or this family," she said.

"Ken, we are grounding you for two weeks. That means you won't be using your car, so hand over your car keys, please."

"Yes, Dad. Yes, Mom," Ken said as he crushed out his cigarette, but there was little respect in his tone. He reached into the side pocket of his jeans and pulled out the wanted key ring. This he handed to Da. "Are you two through now? If you are, I'm going out. This room is too stuffy. I need fresh air."

Mother looked at him, concerned. "Where are you going?"

"To find Bradan. At least he understands me. Wow, will I be glad when it's time for us to leave this little hamlet. This place suffocates me."

"You mean, Forest Lake cramps your style?" Da said.

"Yes. There must be more to life than what this community and family has to offer."

Martha gasped. Across the table, Martin's eyebrows went up. Mother pressed a hand to her brow and looked about to cry. Da looked stunned, as if Ken had actually hit him. Martha could hardly stand the look of pain in her parents' eyes.

"I thought you liked it here in Forest Lake," Martha said.

"We may not have a lot of money," Martin started, "but Dad has provided a good life for us."

"Oh, yeah, yeah. I'll be happy when I go out west and train for the police force out there."

"D'you think they want officers who don't follow rules or who can't be relied upon because they're too drunk to do their job?" Da challenged.

Ken was already heading for the door. As he passed the garbage container, he bent and whisked the cigarette pack back into his shirt pocket. He went outside and lit up.

"You will be in church at ten o'clock tomorrow morning," Da said after him, knowing Ken could hear him through the screen.

"Yes, Dad," Ken answered, but Martha knew he didn't mean it—

and she knew Da knew this as well.

"Mother, I'm all done," Martha said as she laid her dishes in the sink. "I'm going to go see Sherry."

Martin smiled and said, "You mean Bradan." He followed her outside.

Outside, Martha and Martin joined Ken under the big shade tree by the corner of the porch. His face resembled a thundercloud.

"That talk with Dad didn't go too well did it?" Martin said in an attempt to lighten the atmosphere.

"He treats me like a seven-year-old. I'm fed up with it all. I'll live the way I want to. I'm going to find my beloved Sherry. And maybe even Bradan."

Ken started down the little slope leading to a lower, open meadow between the house and road.

"I'm coming with you. I want to see Bradan."

"I don't know what you see in that loser," Martin said and there was no mistaking the dislike in her twin's brown eyes.

Ken heard Martin's words and whirled. "Bradan is not a loser."

"Oh, yeah? Then why did he leave the love of his life sitting in the pitch black night, last evening, while he was passed out in your car?"

Ken took a deep breath to curb his temper. "That doesn't mean he's a loser. Bradan is a kind, caring person."

Martin snorted.

"Look, Martin, you can dislike Bradan all you want, but don't you ever run him down in my presence again. Do you hear me?" Ken's blue eyes snapped sparks of anger.

"Yes, Ken," Martin said, losing all desire to be contrary.

"You are just jealous of him because Martha is having a relationship with someone beside you. Are you coming, Martha?"

"I'm coming." Martha followed her older brother across the road.

Ken and Martha paused in the driveway by the side door of Bradan and Sherry's house. Angry voices reached the three outside.

Ken rolled his eyes. "Family relationships don't seem to be faring any better in the Turehue household."

"Aren't you going to go in?" Martha asked.

Ken said, "Naw, what's the use?"

"Are we just going to wait til someone comes out?" Martha asked again.

"I know where Sherry's room is. I'll throw some pebbles against her windowpane. That ought to get her attention."

Martha giggled as Ken picked up a few pebbles, he smiled at her and they laughed together as he rattled them off the glass. Martha saw movement inside and soon her friend appeared at the window. She opened it and leaned out. Martha and Ken smiled up at her.

"Good morning," Sherry said just loud enough for them to hear.

Ken gazed up at her and asked, innocently, "Did I get you up?"

The girls giggled.

"No. But, I haven't been up long. I was just getting ready to go downstairs and face the music. I'm not even sure where Bradan is."

"I didn't come here to look at Bradan's face," Ken said and blew Sherry a kiss. She blew one back at him. "I'd rather gaze at you."

"I hear voices in the kitchen."

"Yeah, doesn't sound too pleasant in there. Come on down."

"All right. I will be right there."

Sherry left her room and quietly started down the stairs. The further down she went the louder the voices in the kitchen got.

Sherry had hoped to sneak past the kitchen, but just as she stepped off the last step, Mrs. Turehue glanced her way.

Rats!

"Sherry," Mrs. Turehue called. "Come in here. Your Da wants to talk to you."

Sherry knew what was coming and thought that Martha should be there, too.

"Just a second mom, Martha's waiting for me outside. She's part of this too." Ken was too, obviously, but Sherry knew asking him in would be a bad idea.

"Are you sure?" Martha asked when Sherry opened the door.

"Yes. I'm not the only one involved in this," Sherry said.

Martha sauntered into the kitchen, right behind Sherry and immediately felt sorry for Bradan when she discovered him at the kitchen table with their parents. The atmosphere was strained, and she knew right away that their Da had been lecturing for a long time. A radio played softly in the background, tuned into the local news. The reporter was talking about the incident at Mr. Greene's.

Martha sat down beside Bradan. Immediately his face brightened and he smiled at her. Martha smiled back and put a hand on his shoulder. Bradan quickly responded by pulling her head closer and kissing her.

"Martha and I waited and waited for you or Ken to drive us home, last night," Sherry said.

Bradan groaned. "Oh no, not you too. Dad told me all about it."

"We also lost our jobs last night because of what you and Ken did."

"That's too bad. I'm sorry to hear that, my precious one. I know how you like working around horses."

Martha knew he was sorry. "There's life beyond Greene's Riding Stable."

"Mr. Greene said last night that he will likely have to shut down the stables," Sherry said.

"Why would he do that?" Martha knew by Bradan's fidgeting that he wanted to get away and light up a smoke.

Sherry told him what Mr. Greene had told her and Martha.

"That's crazy," Bradan snapped.

Mr. Turehue repeated the name. "Taffy? Isn't she the animal that's an accident just waiting to happen?"

"That's her," Bradan said.

"I wouldn't worry over a job that forces you to dress like a man," Mrs. Turehue told her daughter. "Look at what you're wearing."

Martha looked at Sherry's clothes. Her friend had on what the girls wore at work; blue jeans, way too tight, a shirt and western boots.

"Go and change into lady like clothes."

"Yes, right away, Mother," Sherry said. She was on her feet in an instant. Martha followed, but caught Bradan's smile and his expression that said, "So they are on your back today, too."

In her room, Sherry shut the door and started changing her clothes.

After pulling on a sensible blouse, she said to her friend, "Martha, I know you put on a front about not being angry with Bradan about abandoning you last night, but underneath I can see that anger simmering. I know I'm right."

Martha nodded, slowly. "Yes. I don't want everyone to know about it. If I got angry and said angry words to Bradan that would just aggravate the situation."

Sherry pulled an ankle-length skirt up around her waist and fastened the snaps. "I agree. That's the way it is with Ken and me."

"Bradan will make a fine Christian, man, husband, and Da once he's through this puberty. And it's my duty as his future wife to show him some understanding and support him. That was not him talking downstairs. I don't believe for one second he doesn't want any more to do with God."

Sherry slipped into her shoes and stood up. "I understand what you are saying and agree. Half the time Ken's misdeeds are brought on by puberty. He is a fine man."

Sherry ran a brush through her hair once and looked at her friend.

"Let's go down and stand behind our intended."

"Gladly," Martha said and was the first out the door and down the stairs.

Back downstairs Sherry asked, "May I go now?"

"You may," replied Mr. Turehue.

Bradan jumped to his feet.

"If she can go, I'm going too."

Martha grinned in spite of herself when Bradan didn't wait for an answer. She knew his head had to be hurting as much as Ken's, yet he dashed outside as fast as he could.

Ken kissed Sherry when they met up with him against the porch wall, his face showed great impatience. "Mom made me change into a skirt."

"Dad gave me a going-over too."

"That's the nature of parents," Martha said lightly. "To scold their offspring now and again."

Martha's thoughts about being cast aside last night melted somewhat in Bradan's arms. Bradan hugged her tightly and kissed her, and her anger melted away completely.

"I forgive you," she told him when her lips were free.

"For what?"

"For forgetting to pick me up, last night."

Bradan slapped his forehead with the palm of his hand. "How could I have been so thoughtless? It slipped my mind. I must'a been really tired."

Martha didn't care to reveal what she knew about the real definition of his tiredness.

Ken looked into Sherry's eyes and said earnestly, "I'm sorry about yesterday's behaviour at Greene's stables."

"And I forgive you," Sherry started to say to Ken, but the idea only made him angry.

"What are you two up to now?"

Chapter Five
The Canoe Ride

"Dad's grounded me like a seven year old," Ken grumbled. "He's taken away my car keys."

Bradan stepped in. "We can use my wheels. It's been sitting there in the yard all this time with plenty of gas."

But, Ken had another plan. "I'm going for a canoe ride. How about you, Bradan? Care to come with me?"

"Certainly," Bradan agreed readily. "It will be a relief to catch the breeze from the lake, instead of sweltering here on land. I will have to ask Dad for the use of his canoe."

"Exactly," Ken said with a snort of disdain. "And of course, I will have to ask Dad's permission to use ours."

He turned to Sherry and was all sweetness and gentleness again. "Will you come for a canoe ride with me, my sweet Sherry?"

"Certainly," Sherry replied.

"How about you, Martha?" Bradan asked.

"Yes." Martha said.

"I'll meet you two down at the docks," Ken said. "Sherry, why don't you come with me and we'll talk to Dad together." He entwined his fingers with Sherry's and the two started towards his house.

They found Pastor Asquinn in his study in the church going over the next day's sermon. Martin stood in the doorway; he'd been talking to

Da before Ken and Sherry arrived. Da was surprised to see his son again so soon.

"Sit down, Ken and Sherry."

Ken held one of the two chairs across the desk from his Da steady and helped Sherry get seated, then sat down in the second chair. Martin remained in the doorway, leaning against the doorjamb.

Without preliminaries, Ken jumped right to the point. "I've come to request permission to use the canoe. I want to take Sherry for a ride."

Da didn't answer immediately. Then slowly and carefully he worded his answer. "I don't think so, son."

Ken swore. Martin, Da, and Sherry, cringed.

"But, Bradan's taking Martha out on the lake!"

Da clenched his teeth, and bit back impatient words.

"Don't shout at me. Then, you and Sherry will have to watch from land."

"That's not fair," Ken said. He knew he was way out of line, but he didn't care anymore even if it was his Da.

"Ken, have you forgotten I just took your car keys away from you? How do I know if you can be trusted in a canoe?"

Ken jumped to his feet. "I don't believe this." He started towards the door.

Thinking his son understood watching from land meant watching from home, Da said, "Wait a minute.

Son, before you go, I have something for you to do."

Ken turned back. "I hope I can handle it."

"I think so," Da agreed.

He opened a drawer in his desk and lifted out an object. Sherry recognized it immediately.

"Take the church's tithing money to the house and put it in a safe place. You know where that is?"

"Yes, Dad, I do."

He took the waterproof moneybag and tucked it behind his belt and covered it with the bottom of his T-shirt.

Sherry got to her feet and followed him out. Martin stepped out of the way to let them through. He followed Sherry as Ken hurtled out the door and down the steps.

"Come on," he said to her when at last he paused to talk to Sherry.

"Bradan and Martha are likely already out on the lake."

He took Sherry's hand in his and again, then started towards the lake. Martin followed until he came to the front lawn, then stopped and watched. Ken didn't slacken his pace at all as he passed the house, went down the hill, across the road and the railroad crossing, then down the hill on the other side, and finally ending up at the dock. Martin turned and went inside.

Bradan and Martha were, indeed, already there, like she had heard Ken say they would be. Like Martha, Sherry wore a large straw hat to keep the hot sun off her head and she wore clothes over her bathing costume. Bradan wore only his swim trunks.

"You already have your canoe in the water," Ken said in amazement when he saw the green, wooden canoe bobbing up and down on the waves. The red canoe he would be using was still up on blocks where it always rested when not in use.

"With all the necessary equipment loaded," Bradan said, jovialy. The paddles and life jackets rested on the floor. Bradan's sneakers and clothes were neatly folded into a cushion on the seat. Bradan looked quizzically at Ken.

"Is everything okayed by your Dad, Ken? Did he say you could use the canoe?"

"Of course he did."

Bradan heard his friend's words with apprehension. He glanced at Ken and a little smile passed between Ken and Bradan.

"Bradan, please help me put our canoe in the water," Ken said.

"Okey dokey." Bradan grabbed the bow of the red craft, a wooden cedarstrip, Martha took the stern, and Ken the middle, and soon the canoe sat in the water next to Bradan's boat. Straightening up from securing the canoe to tie spots, Ken was aware for the first time that his brother was right there amongst them. He stared at Martin for several seconds.

Martin moved closer to Ken and said, "Ken, it's not true. You didn't get Father's okay to use the canoe."

"So what if I didn't? Does he think grounding me so I can't go anywhere is going to help? I'll get so bored I'll get into mischief just to stay sane."

"I hear you, Ken," Bradan said

"Twenty years old and grounded," Ken grumbled. "And why

should I have to ask Dad's permission to do anything anyway?"

"I've asked the same question myself lot'sa times," Bradan said.

Bradan turned to Martha. "Okay, get in."

He rested a hand on each of her shoulders and held her steady while Martha stepped aboard. Then as she settled in the bow seat Bradan held onto the side of their canoe to steady it, then Bradan jumped lightly into the stern seat, picked up a paddle and with the sweetest of smiles, said to Martha, "Here's your paddle, my Precious One."

Martha took the paddle, and Bradan quickly picked up the second.

"Start paddling," Bradan said.

"As you say, sir," Martha bantered back.

As one, the two dipped their blades into the lake's surface and the craft glided smoothly away from the dock before Ken and Sherry were properly settled in their canoe.

As the canoes started on their way, Martha marvelled at how smooth the water in Wan Asquinn was. The canoe slipped through the water swiftly, and with only occasional use of the paddles. The canoe glided towards Fifth Point.

With a splash Bradan dipped his paddle into the water. Beyond was the main body of the lake, the surface choppy with whitecaps. Martha and Bradan were just about at the point when she saw Ken's canoe glide up on their right, out of the corner of her eye.

The four canoeists paddled for a little distance, when she noticed Bradan focused intently on Ken and Sherry. She changed her line of vision to Ken's canoe. Bradan grinned broadly but she didn't catch on as to the reason right away.

Then she noticed Sherry struggling with her paddling and that the craft had become almost impossible for her to steer. Martha held a hand above her eyes to shade her eyes from the glare of sunlight off water only to see her sweetheart bursting with laughter. Martha looked back at Ken and Sherry, and saw her brother seated on the bottom of the canoe with his back against the seat, and his head resting on his arms. He used his arms as a cushion for his head. His paddle rested on the floor beside him. He sighed.

"This is the life. I could stay out here where it's so peaceful and the breeze is cool for the rest of my life."

"Clowning around again," Martha said. "May God keep the two of you safe."

Martha thought it was all a joke and burst out laughing at the picture and the look on Sherry's face; but Sherry did not laugh.

"Ken, you lazy low life." She used her paddle to direct a wave of water towards Ken, drenching him.

"Hey!"

"Now you've done it," Martha said to Sherry.

Ken continued, "Sherry, I am not was not used to being called names as you just did, nor am I used to being treated like this. My siblings have been taught to respect the fact that I am chief of the Asquinn clan and my instructions carried out. It isn't wrong to expect my future wife to also treat me with greater respect."

Ken wriggled back up onto his seat. "I can't wear my clothes now, they're soaked. I will have to take them off and wear only my swim trunks, like Bradan."

Ken started to pull his T-shirt over his head. As he did so Martha heard something fall.

"Something fell from your belt," she said. "I saw whatever it is hit the side of the canoe and bounce into the water."

Her eyes scanned the churned up waters. In the stern, Bradan also scanned the water with his merry brown eyes. In the second canoe, Ken and Sherry also searched the water's surface.

By now, without any steering, both canoes had drifted further and further into the main body of the vast expanse of water that was Lake Forest. They bobbed on bigger waves. And huge waves they were, Martha noticed; white caps whipped up by a strong wind that blew constantly and with even stronger gusts at times.

"There it is," Martha said, pointing.

"It looks like the pouch Pastor Asquinn puts the church's tithing money in to take to the bank," Bradan said. "How come you have that, Ken?"

Ken groaned. "Dad gave it to me to take to the house before I came out on the lake."

"Instead of going canoeing," Bradan said.

"I was so angry with him I forgot all about it."

"Uh oh," Bradan said.

"Now I've really done it."

"You lost the money you assured Dad he could trust you with," Martha said.

Ken was distressed. "We've gotta find it. I won't be able to go home without it."

"Exactly what was in the pouch?" Bradan asked. "If there's coins, then the pouch could sink and never be recovered in these deep waters."

"I think there were only bills and checks," Ken answered. "It didn't feel heavy enough to be holding coins."

"It will keep floating then and be washed ashore somewhere," Bradan said.

"There it is," Martha cried, catching sight of the pouch bobbing on a wave crest.

"Good girl," Ken said. "We can paddle over there and pluck it out of the water. I have nothing to worry about. Let's get paddling, Sherry, you on the left and me on the right."

At that moment a strong gust of wind roared by so that Sherry only heard, "...Paddle...", so she ended up putting her blade in the water on the same side as Ken.

Icy fingers ran up and down Martha's spine when the two made a stroke, and Ken received the exact opposite results he wanted. The canoe turned completely around and faced in the opposite direction than that in which the pouch drifted.

"No, no, the left. Paddle on the left, you crazy woman. Now, you've really lost the money," Ken lamented.

"I? I made you lose the money? I couldn't see you to know what side you were paddling on."

Martha glanced back at her sweetheart as he answered for his friend, surprised he wouldn't defend his own sister.

"Yes, you did. He plainly instructed you to paddle on the left."

"You're lucky we didn't end up in the water ourselves," Ken said.

"That wind is really strong now," Bradan said. "These swimming trunks aren't enough. I'm going to put my clothes back on."

Martha made sure she kept her eyes to the front as both boys climbed back into their clothes, pulling them on over their swim wear, except for their sneaker, which remained on the bottom of the canoes.

Ken looked at Bradan. "Did you bring along anything good to

drink?" Martha was glad, when Bradan shook his head.

"I didn't have time to get some."

"Good for you, Honey," Martha said.

Ken looked annoyed. He said in amazement, "I don't know what possessed you to come out on the lake with nothing to drink. I guess lake water will have to do when I get thirsty enough."

"That wind is really strong now," This swimming trunk isn't enough. I'm going to put my clothes back on. I need them to keep warm."

Martha made sure she kept her eyes to the front as both boys climbed back into their clothes, pulling them on over their swim wear, except for their sneakers. Both pairs remained on the bottom of the canoes.

Ken applied the same trick with his friend as Sherry had with him. Soon splashes of water passed between the canoes. This of course added more waves to the ones already buffeting them.

Sherry screamed and Martha saw the canoe tip. The next thing she knew Sherry and Ken were splashing around in the deep, cold water. She called to Ken and pointed. She watched in dismay as his running shoes floated away on the waves. All they could do to save themselves was grab onto the canoe and drift with it.

Martha called to Ken and pointed. She watched in dismay as his running shoes floated away on the waves.

Bradan and Martha didn't remain upright for long either, as another wave hit their canoe, and Martha screamed as the canoe tipped and slowly rolled. The results were two overturned canoes and four young people in the water.

Slowly, the canoes drifted in the strengthening wind and waves. Sometimes the waves were so high so that when they were down in a valley, Martha could not see anything but water and whitecaps; but when they were lifted up on the crest of a wave she could see quite a distance.

"Let's tie these canoes together so we won't drift apart," Bradan suggested. He grabbed the rope on the front of his canoe and threw it to Ken, who caught it. Martha watched, shivering in the icy cold water, as Ken tied the rope together with the one on the front of their canoe and did the same with the back.

"I need a picker-upper," Ken said.

He reached in his shirt pocket for his cigarette package. Martha almost shouted with joy when his hand came back with a soggy mess, which he held this up for all to see.

"These are following our shoes to wherever they chose to drift," he said. Martha couldn't help but feel like hugging him when he tossed them over his shoulder as far as he could.

Martha looked around. "Has anyone seen the church's money pouch?"

Bradan shook his head.

"Not me," Sherry said.

"Nor me," Ken said. "Oh, what have I done?"

Martha glanced at Sherry. Her lips were moving, her eyes closed.

"Are you shivering?" Ken asked, his tone concerned.

Sherry shook her head.

"She's praying," Martha said.

"How female," Bradan said. Martha was so angry she felt like turning around and smacking Bradan with her paddle, but stayed put.

"And you two ought to, too," she said instead.

"Oh don't bother me about praying," Ken said. "God doesn't answer anyway, so why bother?"

"If something happens it would happen that way with or without prayer," Bradan said.

"I'm still praying that God will give me the strength to hang on to this canoe until He sends a rescue boat," Sherry repeated stubbornly.

"And so will I," Martha backed her friend up.

"Okay," Bradan said.

The group fell silent, and the canoe drifted with the waves.

"I'm getting tired," Martha said. "I don't know how much longer I can hang on."

"Please, hang on," Bradan said.

"I'll try." Suddenly, a wave ripped the rope from her weakening fingers. She yelled as she grabbed for something else to grip.

"Here, hold on," Bradan said, offering Martha his hand. She grasped it, but her numb hands could not keep a hold and she let go.

"Bradan, help me." Her scream was cut off as her head slipped under the water.

Chapter Six
Stranded

Holding her breath, Martha tried kicking her feet and hands, but the cold water had numbed her beyond movement, and she headed deeper into the cold water. Down under the churning surface the water was calm and clear. Down, down she went, ever closer to some jagged rocks.

Beneath the lake's surface she could plainly see Bradan as he dove deep, and she was amazed, and a little afraid, at how far she had sunk. Could he reach her, she wondered? He was certainly going to try, she knew this for certain, as closer and closer he came. She was glad he hadn't waited to see if she was a strong enough swimmer to make it to the surface, and came to find her. At last just when she feared he would have to return to the surface for air, he reached out and grabbed her blouse, then he started for the surface as fast as he could, towing her along. The two of them broke the surface a few yards from the canoe, with Martha gasping for air. Ken and Sherry clung to each other, both anxiously watching for them as they reached the surface. The next thing Martha knew, her brother had left the safety of the canoe and swam strongly through the water towards her and Bradan. The rough waves gave him a hard time at first, sweeping him backwards, instead of forwards, but at last he reached his sister's side. He grabbed Martha's other shoulder and together he and

Bradan directed Martha back towards the canoe.

Martha looked back at the canoe for something Sherry could throw for them to cling to. The only thing her eyes could pick out was the rope holding the canoes together.

"That will have to do," she said and called weakly to her friend. "Grab the rope and haul the second canoe close to the one you are holding onto, then untie the ropes and throw us the one tied to your canoe, then haul us in." Sherry did so and the waves spun the second canoe away. Seconds later, the life line, which Sherry had thrown, landed with a splash inches from her.

Martha grabbed the rope. "Good girl," she praised Sherry when she and the boys arrived at the canoe. "I don't know if we would have made it back here without your quick and actions."

"We have only the one canoe, but that's better than nothing," Ken said.

Martha clung to the bow of the canoe; Bradan kept his body close to her in order to keep her warm, and rubbed her numb hands.

"How are you now, my precious one?"

"Much better, Bradan, my handsome one."

Bradan kissed her. "I don't know what I would have done if anything happened to you," he said, a break in his voice. "I wouldn't know how to live without you."

Sherry and Ken clung to either side of the pointed back of the canoe.

Martha suddenly shouted. "I see something."

"A rescue boat like you prayed for?" Ken inquired, skeptical.

"I'm afraid not," Martha had to admit.

Bradan looked disappointed. "Why isn't it a rescue boat? I guess God didn't hear your prayer after all."

The scorn in his voice cut deeply into Martha's feelings, but she said respond. Instead, she said, "It looks like the waves are crashing against an island or something."

"Where?" Ken asked.

Martha pointed.

"Let's try and steer this cumbersome craft towards our paradise island," Ken said.

The four young people paddled with their hands as paddles and did manage to direct the canoe's towards the reef

They were only a few yards away when Ken cussed loudly. "This isn't much of a refuge."

Bradan agreed. "It's only a reef. The way the waves pound against it, we won't be any safer there than hanging onto these canoes." He, too, cursed their luck. "God could have done much better."

"Maybe we should pass it by and look for a bigger island with trees for shelter," Ken said.

"Please don't pass this reef by," Sherry pleaded. "I'm cold and my hands are numb."

Ken sighed and Bradan rolled his eyes.

"All right," Ken said.

The canoe had drifted up to a long, narrow rocky ridge. The boys helped their sweethearts climb onto the reef, and then followed.

Without any weight to hold it down in the water, the canoe drifted away and out of reach, and onward from there, leaving them all technically shipwrecked.

"We are really stranded now," she said. She looked around. White birds with black wing tips circled and mewed in the air.

"I feel like a seagull perched on this narrow ledge," Ken said.

"The seagulls are in the air," Bradan grinned.

Waves crashed against the rocks, then retreated back into the lake, exposing more rocks as it did so.

"Look, there's more of this reef beyond this rock," Sherry said. "We would be more comfortable over there."

Martha looked. Sure enough a layer of rock still showed above the water's surface.

Ken sniffed at the idea. "Rock. I wouldn't call that being comfortable."

But Bradan disagreed. "Maybe she's right. We would have more room to move, at least."

"Ffaen, no problem at ol," Ken said, reverting back to his native Welsh language on purpose. Only Martha knew what he said.

"How do we get across?" Bradan asked.

"There is a ledge here in front of us that leads to those rocks over there," Martha said.

"The water can't be any more than ankle deep," Bradan pointed out.

"Cwm," Ken said to Sherry.

She didn't understand what he wanted. She also knew he was teasing everyone by talking in Welsh. She looked at him strangely.

"I will help you across," he said, "Be careful, the rocks could be slippery."

Leaning on Ken for support, Sherry carefully picked her way across. Her feet slipped once, but Ken caught her.

Bradan and Martha were safely across.

"Da iwan," Ken said to them.

"What does that mean?" Bradan wanted to know.

"Very good," Ken explained. He whispered to Sherry. "See how we can work together as a team."

Sherry nodded. "Yes, Ken."

He was subtle about it, but Martha realized he referred to the fact if Sherry had listened more closely in the canoe they would not be in this predicament. Ken turned away from Sherry and said loudly, "Now, we wait for the girls' miracle rescue boat to show up."

"I'm going to make myself as comfortable as possible on those rocks," Bradan announced. "I didn't get much rest last night and I've had a long day."

"I don't think any of us did and we all have," Ken said. "I know it is uncomfortable, but it's better than standing here watching that storm. Maybe it won't even reach us."

"It will be cool on these rocks once the sun goes down." Bradan reminded everybody.

Ken moved closer to Sherry. "The only way we will have any chance to survive is for all of us to snuggle up together. I know how we can make the night more exciting."

He kissed her. But instead of pulling away, he kept kissing her and moved his body closer to Sherry's.

"Ken, stop that," Sherry told him.

Ken drew quickly away from her, annoyed. His lips turned downward in scorn. "Oh no, don't expect you to give up your puritan ways so we can have a more comfortable night."

Bradan had taken this all in and couldn't remain silent. He stepped between his sister and Ken.

"That's enough. These girls are both ladies and we should be thankful for that. There's plenty of the other kind out there. If you go any further than you just did outside the bounds of marriage with my sister, I will personally drown you."

Ken didn't back down easily. "And if you go any farther with my sister outside the bounds of marriage, I will personally drown you."

"Then we understand each other," Bradan said. "These are fine, well-bred ladies."

Ken turned away.

"Are you boys fighting?" Martha said.

"Not at all," Bradan said.

"Never mind," Ken said. "Good-night, all of you. Watch your step in the dark. This reef isn't very large and I don't want anyone to fall off the edge. The water must be twenty feet deep out there."

The boys tried to go to sleep.

Ken sighed loudly. "It's going to be a long night: nothing to drink, smoke or any kind of comfort. Oh, man!"

Martha remained by the edge of the reef where the group had stood and viewed the storm clouds. As they approached in the gathering dusk, the clouds and lightning seemed even more sinister. They loomed on the horizon like an omen. Martha had a feeling of a coming catastrophe.

Sherry joined her. Martha knew immediately something bothered her friend—and it wasn't the coming storm. She was shaking

"What's wrong?"

"The tiff between your brother and Bradan."

"Bradan loves you as his sister and was merely protecting you."

"It's not Bradan that worries me. I'm not sure how Ken is going to take my brother's interference. Maybe he will consider me too tame and boring, and leave me for someone more his style."

"What do you mean his style? You are his style. I don't think he will resent Bradan's actions, or you. I'm right. I know it. Wait and see."

An unusual, uncomfortable silence fell between the two friends. Finally, Sherry asked, "What were you doing when I joined you?"

"I 'm asking God to turn that storm away from here."

"I'll join you."

"Father in Heaven," Sherry prayed, "that looks like one wicked storm coming our way and will be here before thirty minutes goes by and we have no shelter. We will be lucky to survive. I also pray about the money Ken lost and pray that we will find it No one but you knows where it is at this moment.

"For a while now Ken has not been living a life honourable to you. Please, if it has to be, take mine. I'm ready to go to heaven; Ken has a lot more preparation. Please turn this storm away and cause it to go elsewhere. Amen."

"And Bradan has not lived for you for a few years now," Martha began. "For his sake, and his parents' sake, turn this storm elsewhere so that he can live, and be restored to his once joyful fellowship with you. Amen."

Bradan's voice came to Martha out of the thick darkness on the reef. "Are you girls going to stay there all night and watch that storm?"

Martha turned to face the boys who were snuggled together on the rocks.

"Come on in where it's warm or would you rather talk to God who doesn't exist?" Ken mocked.

"Come on, let's go to bed," Martha said.

When the girls reached the boys resting on their rocky bed, Martha snuggled beside Bradan and next to them, Sherry cozied up to Ken.

From the girls' bedroom window, Martin looked out at Wan Asquinn. Faith was alone in the room; she'd cried out in her sleep, and Martin had rushed into the bedroom.

From the looks of the sky, he knew they were in for one whopper of a storm. He'd never seen such blacks and purples in storm clouds like that before. Those clouds would likely contain hail. Martin heard a faraway rumble of thunder and saw a brilliant and dramatic flash of lightning. His face fell, as he thought about Martha. Did she have shelter for the night?

Faith stirred in her bed.

"Martha," Faith cried out.

Martin knelt at her bedside and hugged his young sister.

"Shushhhh, now. Don't be frightened." Martin wondered about Martha, and Ken, and Sherry, and Bradan. I pray those four have shelter or they will be sitting ducks. A crash of thunder and lightning lit up the darkness. He and Faith exchanged uneasy glances. He feared for his brother and sister, Sherry and Bradan, and he trembled with fear the more he thought. *I hope he hasn't forgotten how to turn situations like this over to God and let Him handle it. He can take care of circumstances well beyond anyone's imagination.*

A sudden sad thought occurred to him. *Or maybe God's reason for sending this storm is to punish Ken for taking the Lord's money.*

Da and Mother had discovered later that afternoon that Ken had not deposited the bag of money as he had said he would. Martin looked down at Faith who had fallen asleep in his arms. Gently, he lowered her head to the pillow and pulled the covers around her then returned to the window and pulled back the curtains and looked down the hill at Wan Asquinn, as smooth as a mirror.

The sun was about to set, and the wind had died down. But, he felt all wasn't as calm as it looked. He noticed storm clouds to the northwest.

He could feel Martha's presence as if she were right there in the room with him.

"Is everything all right, Martha," he said softly. "Faith cried a little bit when she discovered she's alone in this room, but she's okay now."

Martin looked behind him at Faith. She lay in her bed, snoring gently. He turned away from the window, and instead of returning to his own room, flopped down on Martha's bed and he, too, was soon sound asleep.

Chapter Seven
God Turns the Storm Away

Martha didn't know how many hours later it was when she awoke. She pushed herself up on her elbows and listened. She had to shake her head to clear her mind and remember where she was. Not a sound from the storm.

"Pssssst, Ken, are you asleep?" she heard Bradan whisper.

"No, but at least I'm warm," Ken said.

"Listen. Hear anything?"

There was a rustling as Ken sat up. "No."

"Exactly. That storm should have been here by now."

Ken looked towards the horizon. "I don't see any sign of it."

"The stars are shining," Bradan said.

"There's enough light now to see that there isn't a cloud in the sky," Ken said. "Maybe the storm did hit us. Maybe we're all dead and sitting up there on another planet looking down on earth."

Martha held a hand over her mouth to stifle a snicker, but Bradan's laugh bubbled over.

"I don't think so. I feel alive. The storm must have gone around us. Wow, are we lucky or what?"

"Our God kept us alive overnight," Martha said.

"Maybe a draft higher in the atmosphere turned it in another direction," Ken said.

Martha stirred. "Daylight is starting to creep in. I'm getting dressed." She got up and groped around in the shadows. She stubbed her toe on stone. "Ouch!"

Her cry of pain startled Sherry. She sat up. "What?"

"It's nothing, dear," Ken urged.

"Nothing?!" Martha exclaimed. "My toe hurts terribly."

"Time you girls got dressed," Ken said.

"At least our clothes are still with us," Sherry said.

"And dry," Martha added, and pulled her dress over her head, then found some shoes.

"You two didn't lose your hats, even," Bradan commented.

After the girls dressed, Ken said, his tone full of sarcasm, "Now we sit like a colony of seals and wait for our divinely sent rescue boat."

"I prayed all night for God to send a rescue boat, and early enough for us to be in the services this morning. Da did order us to be in church this morning," Martha said. "And when he speaks, as the patriarch of the Asquinn family, speaks we all listen," Ken said in the same sarcastic tone.

Martha said, almost in tears, "I hope Dad never hears me talk like that. I don't want you hear you run down Mam or Da. Da is a wonderful Da and provider, and Mam's a wonderful mother."

"Martha and I prayed for the storm to pass us by, and it did," Sherry said.

"If you girls don't stop being so silly, I'll jump in the water and swim ashore," Ken said. He paused for effect then continued, "then come back with a boat to rescue you."

"You aren't serious, Ken. You will not make it all the way to the mainland," Sherry said.

But, Martha knew her brother well enough to know he could do most anything against the most adverse circumstances, and make it work.

Bradan checked his wristwatch. "Of course he can't. He will stay right here with us and wait. It is now six o'clock."

The waiting began. Seven o'clock. Seven-thirty. Eight o'clock. Nine o'clock.

"I see something," Martha suddenly shouted.

"So did I," Sherry said. She almost danced with joy.

"Where?" Ken and Bradan asked together.

Sherry pointed towards Fifth Point which they had to pass to get into the main body of the lake. "There."

The boys strained their eyes to see what the girls had seen.

"I don't see anything," Bradan said. "It must have been your imagination."

"I saw a flash of light right by that point of land," Martha insisted.

"Well, whatever it was doesn't appear to be there now," Ken said.

"It was probably just a fish jumping for breakfast," Bradan said.

The four settled down to wait some more. Moments later, Ken was on his feet.

"You girls were right," he shouted. "There is a boat on the lake and headed for the south end, but not in the boat's view."

Bradan jumped up and stood beside his friend. His eyes followed the direction Ken looked until they settled on a fishing boat bouncing along on the waves, down the middle of the lake.

"Whoever it is will miss us if we don't do something to attract his attention," Martha said.

"Let's find the highest point and shout and wave our arms," Sherry said.

Ken snorted and swept his hand toward the reef. "There is no highest point."

"But we can still jump around, and wave, and shout," Bradan said.

The group waved and shouted until Sherry's arms ached and her voice went hoarse.

To their relief, the boat changed direction and started towards them.

"Whew," Sherry said. "At last."

"Don't stop," Martha pleaded. "We don't want him to think that we're just an illusion."

The boat remained on a steady course towards the reef. The figure driving grew bigger and bigger until Martha could make out her twin.

The four young people made their way through the shallow water back to where they had first climbed onto the jagged rocks of the reef.

When Martin shut off the motor the silence was almost deafening. He allowed the boat to drift for a while, then picked up a paddle and guided the craft towards them.

Once within talking distance, Martha said, "What are you doing out on the lake so early on a Sunday morning?"

"I could ask you guys the same thing."

"We got stranded," Martha replied, her face reddened with shame. "Our canoe overturned on us, and then they both drifted away."

Martin looked angrily from Bradan to Martha, then from Ken to Sherry. Martha quickly guessed his thoughts.

"There was nothing like that," Martha said.

"Of course not," Martin heckled. "Why would I even think such a thought?"

"I don't know," Martha said.

"There's no reason to," Ken backed up his sister.

Martin switched topics. "You shouldn't have been canoeing yesterday afternoon. Didn't you know there was a small craft warning in effect? That means anything smaller than a cruiser is to stay off the lakes."

Martha said through an impatient sigh, "We all know what it means. We didn't hear about any warning." After a pause, Martha continued, "The water is about thirty feet deep here. There's no fear of hitting rocks if that's why you are afraid to come closer."

The boat came up alongside the rocks. Ken grabbed the front end while Bradan held the back steady.

Ken took Sherry's hand in his and helped her to be seated. Bradan placed a hand around Martha's waist and helped her into the boat and sat down beside her. Bradan and Marta settled in the seat near the front while Ken and Sherry accepted the bench in front of Martin.

"You don't happen to have cigarettes, do you?" Bradan said.

Martha could see Martin's anger boiling at the question.

"Of course not," Bradan said. "You would never do anything like smoke a cigarette." Bradan paused and swept his eyes over Martin, taking in his rigid stance and unsmiling face. "Martin, why don't you relax a little and live?"

Martin's lips tighten in anger and he moved to sweep the boat paddle in the lake and drench Bradan with water, but Ken intervened.

"Come on, Martin. Hurry up and get this boat moving. We need to get home."

Martin resisted the urge to soak Bradan, started the engine and pointed the boat towards Wan Asquinn.

"Did you see anything of a storm last night?" Martha said over the noise of the motor.

Her twin glanced at her, surprised she even knew about the storm, but, said, "What storm?" Martin did not want to tell them about the storm and the damage. They would see the destruction it left behind when they reached shore.

"We saw storm clouds as the sun was setting," Bradan said. "We wondered where the storm went."

Martin didn't reply.

The dock came into view, and as the boat approached, Martha gasped. Small trees had been pounded to the ground. The tips and branches of bigger trees lay everywhere. Ruined boats sat in the water. The roof on the storage shed was pounded in.

Martin watched as the four looked around in amazement at the destruction.

"Wow!" They all muttered.

"What happened?" Sherry asked.

"You asked if we heard anything about a storm," Martin said. "This is where it hit. There's more; some houses were damaged when high winds and hail blew trees down on them and cars parked in the driveways. Basements were flooded. We are lucky."

Martin looked at his watch and grinned back at four weary faces. "We might make it in time to attend the first service. It's 9:45."

Ken nodded, but to Martha it didn't appear that he cared whether they were in time or not.

"All I have to look forward to is disapproval from Dad over losing the money."

Martin guided the fishing boat expertly around the broken dock. Martha grabbed one of the stop cleats on the deck and held the boat steady until Ken was able to jump out.

"Here you are," Martin said. "Safe and sound."

Ken steadied the boat while Martha, Sherry and Bradan scrambled out. Bradan helped Martin secure the craft.

"We have to get to the church," Ken said.

"Let's hurry," Bradan urged.

"But I want to change my clothes," Martha said. "And my hat. I managed to hang onto this straw hat but it isn't suitable for church."

Sherry looked down at crumpled and dirt streaked attire. "I have to agree with Martha. This dress is wet, wrinkled and otherwise filthy. I wouldn't be caught dead in church wearing a hat like this."

"There's no time to go home and change," Martin said. "You girls will have to attend just the way you are."

Ken looked down at his and Bradan's feet. "At least you're wearing shoes."

They had walked in the grass with no incident, but the road, which was covered with cinders, was a different story. Small stones and cinders cut into the soles of the guys' feet as they walked.

"Ouch!" Ken cried and let out a string of curses as he stumbled, twisting his ankle, and falling to the ground. They all rushed to Ken's side.

"Let me examine your foot," Bradan said. Ken lifted up his foot and Sherry grasped it and turned it so she could examine the bottom.

"There's no break in the skin, just a nasty bruise and some swelling."

They helped Ken to his feet and started walking again. Ken did all right until they came to the railroad crossing. Ken's sore foot gave way again and as he stumbled his foot got caught between a slat in the crossing and the rail. Both boys cursed this time.

"Are you all right?" Bradan asked.

"I don't think so," Ken replied through grit teeth. "Now I've hurt my ankle."

"Can you stand up?" Sherry said, concerned.

"I don't know."

Ken tried, but the foot trapped between the rail and the railroad tie prevented him from rising.

"There isn't a train due right away, is there?" Martha said.

"Not at this hour," Bradan said. "Trains go through here either early in the morning or later in the afternoon."

Sherry opened her mouth to say, "Good", but before she could utter the word a train horn blasted the air.

"Oh, no," she said instead, as they all looked at each other in horror.

"The train can't be any farther away than the bridge over the river,"

Martha said.

Bradan carefully tried working his friend's foot loose. He remained calm and relaxed, but Ken did not. He was in a foul mood.

"Come on, Bradan! Can't you get my foot loose?"

"I could if you would keep still," Bradan said.

The next whistle blast was much closer.

Martha jumped up and down in her agony. "Come on Bradan; can't you free my brother's foot? Oh no, we will not get to church on time."

"Is that all you can think of?" Ken said.

A green and orange diesel rounded the curve half a mile away and was thundering towards them.

Sherry finally positioned Ken's foot in a way that would release it from between the ties, but Ken kept moving, and his foot ended up trapped again

"Keep still," Sherry said, sternly as the train's wheels clacked against the steel rails towards them. Urgent horn blasts echoed through the air.

With one final effort, Sherry pulled Ken's foot free. Bradan grabbed him and flung them both into the ditch along the right-of-way. Martha, Martin, and Sherry scurried away to a safe distance on the road. Martha could feel the heat from sparks and cinders that flew into the air from the train's wheels and landed close to where she lay, and the ground shake beneath her.

As the train proceeded farther down the line, Ken pushed himself to his feet. He would have fallen again if Sherry hadn't grabbed him and steadied him.

"I will help you get to church," Bradan said.

With Ken leaning on Bradan for support, the group moved forward again.

But their progress was painfully slow. Clock hands ticked towards ten o'clock.

Bradan chuckled.

"What do you find so funny?" Ken said through the pain of his throbbing ankle.

"I can imagine the 'saintly' members' gasp of disgust and exclamations that Ken and I are so drunk we can't even stand without the other's support, if they can see us."

Ken grunted. "Humph, let them think what they want. Can anyone see us from the church?"

"I'm not sure," Bradan said.

The boys had to stop and rest.

Ken looked at his brother, concern in his blue eyes. "Martin, what do you suppose Dad's thoughts are concerning you about now? Wouldn't he be angry about your absence this morning?"

"Probably," Martin answered, trying not to look concerned, but the look on his face betrayed him.

"You girls go on ahead and get there before the service starts," Bradan said. "We will get there as soon as we can."

"But..." Martha began.

"You heard me."

"Yes, Bradan," Sherry said. She touched Martha's shoulder. "Come on."

"And, go straight to the church," Ken said.

"We will join you shortly," Bradan added.

Martha didn't budge. "I'm not going anywhere. I want to stay with Ken."

"Get going," Bradan said.

"Oh for heaven's sake, let them stay," Martin wailed.

"Don't argue," Bradan said to Martin, frustrated. "She is my future wife."

"And she's my twin sister," Martin reminded the older youth.

"She ought to learn to obey me," Baradan said. "I know you had a problem with me and Martha's relationship right from when I first mentioned it; what are you going to do about it? Stop the wedding?"

"Maybe I will," Martin said. "I just might do that."

After a brief rest, the three boys started moving again, but progress was greatly hampered by the gravel and cinder-covered road beneath bare feet, and the pathway up the hill wasn't any easier. At last, they walked past the house and approached the church.

When they arrived at the bottom of the steps, they could hear Pastor Asquinn, through an open window announcing the first hymn and the organ start to play.

Together, Martin and Bradan supported Ken as he hopped up the steps. Sherry held the door open, then followed Martha as Bradan and

Martin helped Ken into a back aisle. Sherry sat down beside him while Martha and Bradan sat down close together. Martin found an empty seat in the pew ahead.

When the first hymn ended the song leader sat down and her Da took his place behind the pulpit.

"First, I want to thank the families that helped us pump out flooded basements last night. There certainly were enough of them and I know very few of us got much, if any, sleep last night."

Chapter Eight
Facing the Music

"I'm here like you ordered me yesterday afternoon to be."

"It doesn't matter what condition you are in; at least you are in church."

Out of the corner of her eye, Martha saw Bradan stir. Once glance at him told her the pastor's words made his blood boil.

"He's not drunk, if that's what you're thinking," she heard him say. She wondered if Bradan hadn't misunderstood the pastor's motive; and besides that he looked like he felt more like screaming his words out, but he kept a rein on his temper.

Bradan defended his friend. "The only liquid we tried not to swallow last night was lake water. Ken hurt his foot. We aren't sure if his ankle is broken or not."

Martha's insides tightened as Da studied first Ken, then Bradan, then her, before returning his attention to the church service.

As the meeting continued, Martha felt her face grew hotter and hotter with embarrassment as Ken's head slumped forward on his chest. She poked Ken in the side with an elbow and he woke up and sat up straight, but within a few moments his head fell forward again. Martha glanced back at Sherry and Bradan and saw that Bradan, too, was asleep.

"Wake up, Ken," Martha said.

Ken looked groggily around, afraid the voice belonged to his Da and a scolding was forthcoming. Ken came awake and sat up. He looked around at an empty auditorium. Da and Martin leaned on the back of the pew, looking down at him.

"Where is everyone?"

"Church is over," Da said. "Mam and Martha went to the house to see to dinner."

"Where's Bradan?"

No one answered him.

Da reached out to assist Ken to his feet. "Let me help you to the house."

Ken brushed him off. "I don't need your help."

A sharp pain quickly reminded him of his ankle and he sat down again. Martin and Da supported Ken on either side as he limped down the aisle, out of the sanctuary, out of the church, into the house. In the living room, Mam talked on the telephone. Finally, they reached the bedroom. The younger children gathered around the door.

"What's wrong with him?" Timmy asked.

Martin lowered Ken onto his bed, while Martha put pillows under his foot to elevate it, and covered him with a warm blanket.

"Mom called Doc Stewart. He will be here shortly," Martha said.

Moments later, Da and Mother entered the room with Doctor Stewart following.

"Good afternoon, Doc," Ken greeted the slightly built man.

"En," their mother gasped, appalled at her son's manners. The doctor didn't seem to mind, though, as he returned Ken's greeting cheerfully. "Now to have a look at that foot."

He turned back one corner of the blanket and reached for the aching ankle. Ken cried out in pain and uttered a curse at his gentle prodding, causing Da to raise one eyebrow and Mother to put a hand over her mouth. Neither of the twins said anything.

"It isn't broken," Doctor Stewart reported. "I see only bruising and swelling. Give your foot plenty of rest, keep it elevated and use crutches to walk with I have a pair of crutches with me that I will give you. Put ice on the sprain for the next three days. I'll wrap your foot now with a tensor bandage."

"How long will I have to rest my foot, Doc?" Ken said.

"A couple of weeks, maybe. I'll want to see you in my office a week from tomorrow."

"He will be there," Da assured the doctor before Ken could say anything.

"Dad, I'm old enough to do my own talking," Ken almost growled.

Da shooed the crowd of children in the room, out so that Doctor Stewart could do his job.

When Doctor Stewart was gone, Mam and Da stayed in the room. Ken looked up at his Da who gazed down at him, his expression unreadable.

Martha didn't know what to think, but thought for sure Da was about to give Ken a long lecture.

"That ankle needs rest now," was all Da said.

But Ken clearly didn't feel like taking it easy, as he struggled to his feet and stood by his dresser.

"What I need is to get cleaned up."

Martha headed for the bathroom to put out clean towels for him.

Later, all clean and refreshed, he hobbled into the living-room where Da, Mam and Martha and Martin sat. Ken found a place to sit down on the couch beside Martin. He rested his injured ankle on the footstool. Mam rose to her feet and left the room, returning shortly with a tea towel full of crushed ice, which she placed on Ken's aching ankle.

"How do you feel now?"

"Much better. Thank you, Mam."

"Good. Then we will talk," Da said.

"Yes, Dad."

"Why you were out on the lake after I specifically said you could not use the canoe?"

Ken swore. "I'm not a child. I don't have to ask permission for everything I do. I am twenty years old."

"You will be twenty years old," Mam corrected.

"Then, act like it," Da added. "As long as you live under this roof you will abide by its rules just like everyone else."

Martha closed her eyes, but sneaked a peek at Martin. She had heard these lines from Da so many times before. So had Ken, and Martha realized why he was having a hard time keeping control of his temper. She leaned against the back of the couch and stared at the ceiling.

"Why were you out all last night?"

"I've been out all night lot'sa times before last night."

"But you weren't with Sherry."

"Nothing happened. I simply took Sherry for a good time on the lake."

"Explain exactly what did happen. Start from where you four ended up in the canoes."

"A big wave swamped the canoe, and the canoe overturned," Ken began. "We were left adrift and drifted for some time. The girls did a lot of praying that a rescue boat would show up and rescue us, but nothing like that happened. We tied the canoes together so we wouldn't get separated, then Martha lost her grip and sank beneath the surface. Bradan dove down after her and brought her back up. I jumped in the water to help when they surfaced. That's when Sherry untied one cane and threw the rope to us. The wind caught the loose canoe and swept it away. That left four of us clinging to one canoe, drifting with the wind. Eventually we reached a reef and in our eagerness to get out of the canoe, it, too, was swept away. We were all wet and cold, so we took our outer clothing off and hung them up to dry. By then we were all exhausted, so snuggled up to stay warm and tried to get some sleep with the threatening storm clouds looming on the horizon."

Martha cut in, "You should have seen those clouds, Da."

"What would be so special about them?" Mam asked.

"White clouds towed high into the sky on top of really, really dark clouds beneath," Martha explained. "I knew a bad storm was approaching with thunder and lightning and hail. And we were on a bare reef with no shelter. Sherry and I stood and prayed that God would turn the storm away," she looked meaningful at Ken. "And he did." Then Martha said, "I remember the boys arguing about something. They were apart from us, so we couldn't hear what they said."

Da looked at Ken. "What did you and Bradan argue about?"

Ken looked embarrassed. "Oh, you know. Sex. Bradan told me if I touched Sherry overnight he would personally drown me, and I told him I'd do the same to him if he touched Martha.

"Anyway, we clung to a reef for survival all night. I was with, Bradan, Martha and Sherry. We lost everything, except the clothes we wore, when the canoe tipped over."

"And the Lord's money?" Da said. "Why didn't you put it safely in the bank like you promised me you would?"

"I forgot." Ken lowered his eyes and looked at the floor in shame.

"Forgot?" Da repeated, sick at heart. Martha felt that one word held in it his feelings about the matter and towards his eldest son. "And I presume it's lost along with everything else?"

"Yes, sir," Ken answered respectfully.

Martha figured it was too late for Ken to get back into his father's good graces by being polite.

"We think the money pouch could be washed ashore anywhere," Martha said.

"And I'm inclined to agree," Da said. "Oh, Ken."

"I'm sorry, Dad." When his Da said nothing, Ken continued, "if only you would smile at me that special little smile you used to, Dad. When you did that I knew you were well pleased with me. You never look at me that way anymore. You aren't pleased with me, are you Dad?"

Da looked at his eldest son. "I wish I could, son. Your actions and your behaviors in the last little while make it very difficult. Your disrespect towards me and your blatant disobedience. Your drinking and driving afterwards. Your putting other people's lives in danger—even that of someone whom you wanted to be your wife. You lost the tithing money—the Lord's money. I gave you a chance to redeem yourself, and you still proved that you're not trustworthy and responsible." Da put his hands on Ken's shoulders. "Please know that you are my son, and I love you no matter what you do. Heaven knows I've done enough sinful things in my time, too, and God the Father loves me anyway. That's the way it is with me and you, Ken."

Da took Ken's keys from his pocket, placed them in Ken's lap, then straightened up. "You have said several times now that there's nothing here for you and how much you want to leave." Martha nearly gasped as she anticipated Father's next words. "Go join your redcoats out west. You seem to think they have more to offer you than anything here at home. I won't stop you. You and Bradan are also no longer members of the Golden Ridge Baptist Church and will remain that way until you both show some repentance. Perhaps the experiences of a police officer will teach you humility and service, rather than the arrogance and selfishness you've shown in the last few years."

Ken slowly picked up and looked at them as if they were some foreign object before pocketing them. "I want to talk to Bradan, now."

"I'm afraid that is impossible."

"Why?"

"He's not welcome here anymore nor are you welcome at his place."

"Bradan and I have shared everything since we came to live here."

"Both families think it's time you boys were separated," Mam explained.

"Furthermore, you won't be seeing so much of Sherry, and only under supervision, until after you graduate Police Academy and are married. Mr. Turehue arranged to do the same with Bradan and Martha," Da finished.

Ken's face turned red with suppressed anger. He set the ice pack aside struggled to his feet. "What a crazy arrangement!"

"We haven't finished talking yet. Where are you going?"

"Out to the porch. I need some fresh air. This house suffocates me. What a tiresome family this is. Forest Lake bores me."

Ken hobbled towards the door into the porch along the front of the house. Martha and Da followed him. Martha made herself comfortable on a wide window ledge. She opened a window, letting in fresh air, when Ken lit up again. He even stood by one of the open windows, thinking the smoke would go outside. He was able to get in two deep drags before his Da plucked the weed from between his fingers and ground it out in a flower pot.

"Did you have to do that?"

"You know the rules."

Ken sighed. "Yeah, yeah."

"Ken, if you don't quickly show a change in attitude I will use the strap on you. You may think you are too old for that, but I wouldn't care if you were eighty. You are rapidly pushing me in that direction. You are correct, son, we don't seem to be able to communicate anymore. We don't get anywhere in our conversations. I have nothing more to say to you. When you get your thinking sorted out come to me then and we'll talk."

Ken said nothing.

Da stalked to the door.

Martha looked at her father, unable to believe what was taking place.

"Da," she called.

Da kept going. Martha jumped from her perch and rushed to Da and grabbed him by a hand and said with a break in her voice. "So, you are kicking him out of the house?"

"Not kicking him out," Da clarified. "Mam and I are simply allowing him to do what he wants. He can stay here until college starts in the fall. We won't put any more restrictions on him."

Ken stood up and went outside. He stumbled down the steps to the front lawn as best he could on his own. On the bottom step he paused to light up. Martha remained in her window seat. Their three younger brothers and sisters round the corner of the house just as Ken reached the ground. They stopped and stared at him with his cigarette.

"What?" He asked sharply.

"Nothing, Ken," Faith said.

"Then go find something else to do and stop staring at me," Ken said.

"You know, you used to be nice to us before you started smoking and drinking," Timmy said.

"Now you're not very nice to us at all," Vince said.

"Come on, let's go," Timmy said. The three youngest siblings hopped and skipped off down the hill.

Ken limped over to the picnic table under a huge birch tree at one corner of the yard. He sat down on the table with his feet resting on one of the chairs. He sat like this, staring across the waters of Wan Asquinn for quite some time thinking, Martha guessed.

Martha moved to the porch door. She went down the steps and joined Ken.

"What errand are you cooking up to send your siblings on this time?" She quizzed Ken with a hint of amusement in her voice.

"None yet," Ken said mysteriously.

"Why not send them to recover the lost money?"

Ken shook his head. "It's impossible. The money's gone. I'll never get it back."

"I'm certain it can be recovered," Martha said, confidently.

Chapter Nine
Tithing Money Recovered

This surprised Ken. "Impossible. I appreciate the thought, sis, but there's thousands of rocks and crevices the money could have been washed ashore on, not to mention the beaches."

Martha shrugged as she stood. "Don't be so sure."

As she headed towards the house, Ken called to her.

"Could you bring me my guitar, please?"

"Sure."

After fetching Ken's guitar, she joined her mother in the flower garden, admiring the colourful blooms that lined the side of the house. Strains of music reached her. Martin, Faith, and Ricky returned from wherever they had scattered off to, laughing and joking, and making a lot of noise in general. Martha looked over at Ken, but he seemed completely focused on his music and didn't seem to notice the racket. So she was surprised when the guitar music stopped and Ken called them over.

"Come 'ere you four."

Martha, Faith, Martin, and Ricky exchanged nervous glances with Mother who nodded, indicating they should go to him.

"What do you want, Ken?" Martha said when they arrived.

"The wind blew yesterday afternoon from the northwest," Ken said no one in particular.

"I wouldn't know," Martin said. "I didn't realize I was expected to keep a record of which way the wind blew from each day."

"Okay. I guess I deserved that from the way I've treated you guys lately, but I'm trying to figure something out here."

"Sorry."

"The wind blew from the northwest," Ken began again. "That means our canoes would have drifted away from the reef towards the bay two down from ours."

"So you think…?" Martha started. Mother's head perked up from the garden and Martha knew she was listening in.

"So, I think," Ken continued, "that there might be a chance of recovering the canoe and the tithing money. There's only one slight problem." Ken lifted his bandaged foot in the air.

"The doctor told you to rest that foot," Ricky said.

"There's no way I could get to it. So you three would have to do it for me."

"But we have church to attend this evening," Ricky said.

Ken made a face. "As if I need reminding. If you left now, you'd have plenty of time to search and get back in time."

"Let's go," Martin said.

"Faith, you stay behind with Ken, and mom," Martha said before following Martin and Ricky.

Martha, Martin and Ricky followed a well-worn footpath through a belt of woods past two occupied summer cottages. The families were out enjoying the summer weather.

"Good Sunday afternoon," Martha said on their way.

"It's a wonderful afternoon."

"If you're not already attending a church, you'd be welcome at our evening service," Martin invited.

"We sure will be out to church this evening."

"It starts at half-past-six," Martha said.

"The white church on the ridge," Martin said.

They walked along the trail further until at the end they came to a crumbling old house.

"Let's stop here and explore," Ricky said.

"No way. We have to keep going," Martha said, "or we'll never make it back in time for evening service."

The trail joined up with a cow path that wound through the woods to another bay and an isolated and little-used swimming beach.

At one spot, the marks of carts from Forest Lake's first settlers, and the occasional more modern car that travelled over the road etched into the sandy ground ran close to one end of a bay of Lake Forest. At the end of the cove was a thick entanglement of underbrush which discouraged a lot of people from getting a closer look at the inlet. Martha knew they would have to go through that brush since it was the only way to get where they wanted to go.

Martha went through first. She stood gaping at the destruction as her brothers joined her.

The water in the bay was shallow with a white sand bottom and huge ragged rocks strewn everywhere. While the water where she and her brothers stood was free of weeds, the far side was full of weeds and bulrushes that had once stood thick and tall.

"Look at that," Ricky said in disbelief.

The weeds had been broken off at right angles, the tops floating on the water's surface. The trees, flowers and grass had also taken a beating.

"Hailstones, I would guess," Martha said.

In a shaded knoll by the tree line some hailstones still remained. They were cool, untouched, not melted by the sun.

"Hailstones as big as golf balls," Martin said, as he picked one up.

Martha shaded her eyes from the bright sun with her hand and looked far out across the lake. Martin did the same.

"Help me, please!" Ricky's voice brought Martha's gaze back to the sandy stretch of shoreline. She looked back at the entanglement of underbrush to see Ricky caught up in some branches and briers of the undergrowth.

"Gosh, Ricky. How are we going to get you free of those brambles?"

Martha worked for a while to loosen a stubborn thorn from the hem of Ricky's tee-shirt. At last the thorn let go and her brother leapt free.

"Is that the reef you guys were stranded on all night?" Martin asked.

"Yes," Martha said. "Sherry and I stood on the edge of that reef and watched that storm and prayed that God would direct the storm elsewhere. Mom told me she did the same at home."

"Hailstones that size would have torn the flesh right off your bones," Martin said in hushed tones. "If it weren't for you and Sherry's prayers, you all would be dead now."

"I know." Martha answered in the same hushed tones in awe of their Creator. "But to save us, Forest Ridge got the storm instead. I've already told Da this, and Ken was there. He will likely laugh me to scorn someday when we are alone."

"God spared his and Bradan's life that night," Ricky said.

"Tell him that and it might be what God uses to bring him back to Him, eventually," Martin said.

A few moments later, Martha noticed something in the water. "Look, what's that?"

Martin and Ricky looked in the direction she pointed.

"I can't quite tell what it is from here," Martha said.

"It's a black, or is it green, heap of debris," Martin said. "Could be one of the canoes."

"Let's go closer," Martha said. Martin and Ricky followed Martha through the ankle-deep water to the pile of debris. Since Ricky was shorter than his older brother and sister, the water came to his knees.

"It's the Turehues' canoe," Martin said as he dragged what was left closer to shore.

"That it is," Martha said.

"And it isn't worth rescuing," Ricky said. "Hailstones pounded holes in the sides and bottom and rocks and waves smashed it up even more."

Martin looked around. "I wonder where the second canoe is?"

"They were tied together so we wouldn't be separated," Martha said. "but in the end, both canoes got away from us."

Martin said, "Dad's canoe could be at the south end of Lake Forest by now."

"Maybe not. Come on, let's hurry to the next bay," Martha said.

Martin and Ricky followed as Martha ran back to the forest trail and followed it. The path here was level and easily travelled, and within ten minutes, they had reached the next bay. Martha stopped where the trail left the woods about half way down the cliff face. Faint marks in the moss covered rocks showed where the path continued upwards to the top of the cliffs and rejoined the forest. In contrast to the openness of the shallow bay they had just left, this one had fifteen-foot granite cliffs that towered above the water. Today, placid waves lapped at the rocks, always deep at the base of cliffs like these, and above were grass and forest.

"Here we are," Martha said.

"But no canoe," Martin said.

"No canoe," Martha repeated. "Perhaps it was even more damaged than the Turehues'."

"Where do we start looking?" Ricky asked.

"We scour all those rocks from right here beneath our feet to yon ung." Martha said, reverting to her native Welsh, and waving her hand, indicating the long finger of land that jutted out into the water forming the mouth of the bay opposite to them.

"That's an awful lot of area to cover."

"Let's get started," Martha said. "We will spread out, but not too far. Keep each other in sight."

Martha, Martin and Ricky started searching the moss-covered ridge of rocks below them. Martha stepped carefully over smaller rocks in her way, and over fallen, dead tree trunks. They had just about reached the middle when Martha stopped. She could see an object resting in the hollow of a rock. The sun reflected off its surface, and she knew it wasn't a rock.

"Hey, guys, come over here." Martin and Ricky scrambled to her side.

Martha pointed. "There. I think that may be it."

"Martha, what colour was that pouch?" Ricky asked.

"Gray, and it's waterproof."

"Well, it certainly doesn't match the rocks around it," Martin said.

"Whether it is or it isn't, we have to take the chance and see what it is," Ricky said.

"The only way to reach it is to continue on down the ledge, which is too narrow for me or you, Martin," Martha said, pursing her lips.

"But not for me," Ricky said, bravely. "I can crawl along that ledge and bring back whatever that object is."

"Are you sure, Ricky?" Martha said.

"Sure, I'm sure."

"Well, go on, then" Martin said.

"And be careful," Martha whispered, "or Mam will kill us."

Ricky planted his feet firmly on the narrow ledge and grasped whatever support he could find from the rocks above his head as the path curved down closer to the water and away from Martha and Martin. Above him, the twins followed his slow progress by creeping along with him as long as they could go. His progress was slow.

Please God, take care of him and keep him from losing his footing and end up in the waves below.

Martha had barely finished her prayer when Ricky shouted from below.

"I've found it."

"Good," Martin said.

"Thank you, Lord," Martha said, clasping her hands and looking up.

"But I can't reach it," Ricky said. "I need a long stick with a hook on the end."

"We will look for one," Martha said.

Martha and Martin left the ridge and headed back along the forest path. It only took a few minutes to find an appropriate stick. Martin picked it up, and they went back to their vantage point above Ricky, where Martin lowered it so Ricky grasp it.

They watched and waited as Ricky attempted to hook the handles of the pouch and lift it up. He tried several times before he succeeded.

"I've got it," he shouted as he lifted the pouch towards them.

Ever so carefully, Martha took the pouch off the stick and secured it to her skirt with one of her shoelaces.

Ricky rejoined them on the wider point of the ridge.

"The waves really must have been gigantic yesterday afternoon," he said, "to have deposited the bag up this high."

"Can the money be used do you think?" Ricky said.

"We will let Dad decide about that," Martha said. "We had better get the money back."

The three started back along the path they had come.

"Do you think returning the money will make Da forgive Ken and let him be a part of our church again?"

"I'm sure Da will forgive him, Ricky."

The sun had not even started its descent in the sky when they emerged from the woods a few yards from the railroad crossing.

Martha suddenly stopped. "Listen."

Martin and Ricky listened.

"Fiddle, and harmonica music," Martin said.

"It sounds like Ken and Bradan," Martha said, confused.

"Weren't those two forbidden to associate with one another?" Ricky asked.

"Yes," Martha replied.

"Let's hurry," Martin said. "I don't want to miss this."

Martha led the way up the hill. She, Martin, and Ricky stopped beneath a huge spreading birch tree lining the driveway to watch and listen.

Ken and Bradan were indeed playing music together and just about every member of the church stood listening, captivated. Sherry sat on the bench around the picnic table. When she saw the three, Sherry got up and walked over to them.

"Did you find it?"

"Yes, we did," Martin reported as Martha showed her the pouch.

"How did they manage to get to playing together?" Martha asked.

"It was Bradan's idea," Sherry said. "He heard Ken practicing his guitar and asked Dad if he could join him. Dad asked your dad, and here they are."

Ken stopped playing the instant he saw why his fiancée left her seat. He and Bradan set their instruments carefully down on the picnic table.

Martha untied the pouch from her skirt band and handed the bag to Ken, but their Da intervened.

"Give that to me."

Martha did. "I hope you're not still mad at Ken."

Da looked at her.

"It was Ken's idea to send us looking for it. He figured out where the storm might have carried it, and that's where we found it. It was all his idea."

Da looked at Ken then back at the money pouch, but didn't say anything.

"Is the money okay?" Martha asked.

"We're about to find out," Da said and turned back to the picnic table. "Could you boys move your instruments aside, please."

When they did he tipped the small gray bag and half a dozen grey tithing money envelopes spilled out onto the table. Most everyone let out an audible sigh of relief to see that the bills and checks inside appeared alright.

"The money and checks inside should be fine," Da said. "All is dry."

Mrs. Asquinn looked at her oldest son. "I would say you are one lucky man."

For once Ken didn't have anything to say. He just nodded and looked down at the ground.

Sherry folded her hands together, "Oh, thank you, God."

The boys cast her, if somewhat begrudgingly, an admiring look.

Da collected the money and returned the bills to the pouch. "I will take charge of that now. Ken, you and I will drive into town tomorrow and take it to the bank."

"Yes, Dad," Ken answered meekly, too relieved that the money was recovered to be cheeky.

Da followed the driveway around to the back and entered the house through the back porch. Mam and Ken exchanged little smiles. The boys' audience, feeling that the music show was over for the afternoon, quickly broke up.

"You are going home now, Sherry, Bradan," Mrs. Turehue said. The four stood together on the little glade above the public parking lot. Ken stood by Sherry's side.

"It's nearly suppertime and then we have church this evening," Mr. Turehue said.

"Yes, Dad. Coming," Bradan answered. "I want to say bye to Martha first."

"Be right there, Mom." Sherry said.

"You don't want to go any more than I want you to leave," Ken said.

"No, I don't. Ken, I love you so much I want to be at your side all the time."

She gazed deep into his blue eyes and Sherry felt herself go helpless and weak at the depth and intensity of the love in his return gaze. It staggered her.

"And I love you," Ken said.

Meanwhile, Bradan took Martha's hand and led her to the other side of the birch tree, about as much privacy as their parents would probably allow. Bradan took her in his arms and Martha gazed lovingly up into his face. Then he kissed her. Something intense flowed between them.

"Oh, Bradan," Martha squealed.

"See you in church, my precious one. I love you."

"I love you, Bradan."

Bradan turned to his sister. "Our parents are waiting."

Ken managed to get in another quick kiss before he and Sherry parted.

Sherry walked beside Bradan ahead of their parents towards home.

Chapter Ten
Change in Plans

Ken shifted in the pew, restlessly. Sherry, who sat beside him, glanced at him. Martha, sitting behind them with the Turhues, looked from Ken to Sherry and wondered what could be wrong. Ken's mind seemed miles away, and not on the service.

The instant church ended Ken hurried, as quickly as he could with his sore ankle, to the back of the church.

"Sherry, darling, I want to apologize for being so irresponsible in the canoe. I should have known better than to fool around getting Bradan wet the way I did. I also want to apologize for being so mean to you. You are not a stupid woman. You are very intelligent."

"Why, thank you, Ken," Sherry answered.

"Will you forgive me, my gentle-mannered Sherry?"

"I forgive you, darling Ken," Sherry answered. "When I think of Colossians 3:12 & 13."

Sherry started quoting the passage, but Ken cut in. "Put on therefore, as the elect of God, holy and beloved, bowels of mercies, kindness, humbleness of mind, meekness, longsuffering forebearing one another, and forgiving one another, if any man have a quarrel against any: Even as Christ forgave you, so also do ye."

Sherry was delighted to hear this from her future spouse. She kissed him. "We are to be patient with one another's faults and not be judgemental," Sherry said. "Romans 14:13 — Let us therefore not judge one another anymore: but judge this rather, that no man put a stumbling block or an occasion to fall in his brother's way."

Sherry was astonished when he asked, "Will you marry me?'

Without a heartbeat's hesitation, Sherry answered. "I sure will. I already said I would, ten years ago."

"I mean immediately," Ken said.

This left Sherry speechless for a while, but she answered. "Sure."

"Good," Ken said happily. "I have a plan, but we will have to talk to my parents first. I'll see you later this evening."

Subtly, Bradan worked his way closer to Ken.

"We will have to think of a way we can be together with our sweeties without our parents around snooping. Why do I have a feeling you are cooking up with a plan so we can be together again?"

Ken didn't answer because Bradan's family had moved towards the door. Bradan quickly moved away from his friend.

The attendees slowly vacated the building. Following each service, church members and visitors socialized and lingered. But this evening, it seemed like they would never leave. Martha could see that this bothered Ken. She felt like screaming herself.

Finally, the door shut and all was quiet. Martha didn't see anything of Da. He was likely in the office talking with someone.

Mr. and Mrs. Turehue moved down the aisle and continued outside.

"We'd better get going," Bradan whispered in his sister's ear. Sherry reluctantly looked at Ken, but obediently followed her brother and parents out.

Martha followed Ken as he hobbled outside and the two of them stood on the step. Rain poured down from the clouds. She huddled with her fair-haired brother under the small roof above the step to keep dry. The rest of the churchgoers had dashed to either their cars or their homes to get in out of the downpour.

With his sprained ankle Ken couldn't hurry anywhere. He stood on the top step, miserable. To ward off depressing thoughts, he reached for his cigarettes and lit up. He had finished it, ground it out and still no one came out the door.

Are we going to be here on the step alone all night? Was there even anyone in the church building? Martha wondered.

Then, the door opened and Da stepped outside. He seemed surprised to see them. He turned and locked the door before speaking.

"Why are you two still here?"

"Nobody offered to help me home," Ken said. "Although I am certain Bradan would have assisted me if he had been allowed to. I didn't want to try and get home on my own in the rain. I'd get soaked. I might catch pneumonia."

"And I'm not strong enough to carry him across," Martha said.

"You could anyway catch cold anyway," Da said. "It would have been better for you to wait inside. It's warm and dry in there." He stopped beside Ken. "If you will allow me to, I can carry you to the house. That would be quicker than you walking."

"I will allow it," Ken said.

Da lifted Ken up in his arms as if he were twelve years old. He moved as quickly as he could in the pouring rain and soon set Ken down in the warmth of the porch. Martha hurried behind.

"I appreciate that, Da," Ken said.

Once in the kitchen, Ken waited made sure the younger children were out of sight in various other parts of the house before approaching his father.

"Da, I want to call a meeting."

Da was surprised.

"A family meeting? Why?"

Ken clarified. "I want to meet with Mr. and Mrs. Turehue, you and Mam and I want the girls to be included. I want to discuss the weddings. I haven't talked to Bradan and Martha, but I'm sure they will agree."

"All right. When did you want this meeting to take place?"

"Immediately. We will meet as quickly as they can get over here."

"I guess that would be okay," Da answered. "Martin!"

Martin appeared in the kitchen a few moments later.

"Yeah, Dad," he said.

"What?"

"Go over to Turehues' and ask if it's possible for them to attend a meeting here this evening. Ken has asked for all of them to come."

"All right, Dad," Martin replied.

Martha was already seated in the living-room watching Atlantic Sound of Music with Danny Dablow when Ken hobbled over to the couch and settled himself to wait for the rest to arrive. He rested his bandaged foot on the coffee table.

The show wasn't quite over when Bradan entered the room. Ken moved over as best he could so Bradan could sit beside Martha. Sherry squeezed onto the couch beside Ken.

"What's up, my friend?" Bradan asked.

"You will find out in a minute," Ken replied.

The adults came into the room and found places to sit down.

"We're all here, Ken," Da said.

Sherry pushed herself off the couch, switched off the TV set, then went back to her seat.

"Thank you, Sherry," Ken said. Then he looked around at the others in the room. "I wanted you all here because I have an announcement to make."

"An announcement?" Martha said. This raised eyebrows throughout the room.

"I want to marry Sherry immediately. I've asked her and she said, yes."

The Turehues were speechless.

Mrs. Asquinn looked devastated. "But, why now, son? You aren't earning your own income, and Sherry isn't finished school yet?"

"This is truly where the trail forks. Da told me that you two decided not to hinder me any longer and to make my own plans. I won't make plans for my future without my beloved Sherry." Sherry stirred beside him. "Are you alright with that, Sherry?"

"The sooner I marry you, the happier I will be."

"But what about your plans tobe a policeman?" Mrs. Turehue asked.

"Won't this pull the plug to all your dreams?" Mr. Turehue added.

"I wouldn't want you to forfeit your dream of being a policeman," Da said. "You have dreamed of being a law enforcement officer since you were old enough to know what you wanted to be when you grew up."

"Not if we do things our way," Bradan said. He looked at Ken, baffled. "What is our way, anyway?"

"We want to get married before I go west to train. I don't want to be without you for however long it takes to complete training."

"And if we can't get married right away, I won't leave Sherry and go thousands of miles away to police academy," Ken added.

Mr. Turehue looked at Sherry, eyebrows close together in anger. "Did you know about this before?"

"Not a word. I didn't hear a peep about his plan until now."

"Nobody did," Ken said. "That's because I didn't know myself what I was going to do until this evening. My plan came to me in church."

"How soon is soon?" Bradan wanted to know.

"As soon as my foot is better. Doc Stuart doesn't expect it to take any longer than five days for my ankle to heal."

"Five days?" Bradan said. "Now look here Ken, let's think this out. Perhaps we are being a bit hasty."

"Five days."

"Five days it is."

"Bradan and I want to get married the same time you do in a double ceremony," Martha said.

"But both of you were so excited over a police wedding," Mrs. Turehue said.

"What will happen now?" Mother asked.

Ken drew Sherry closer to him as he answered, "I can't speak for Bradan or you, Martha, but my Sherry will have to learn to cope with disappointments in life. Both couples will go our separate honeymoons on our way out to the police academy. Sherry loves and trusts me; we all have grown to love and trust each other. Now all I have to do is convince you, and Sherry's Mom and Dad, there will be a wedding in the future and for you to marry Sherry and me. I hope for a double wedding; that Bradan and Martha will agree to marry at the same time."

A hush reigned in the living room.

Mam studied the couple. Sherry snuggled close to Ken. He had one arm around her while she rested her head on his chest. The love that flowed between them and the love light shining in their eyes was very evident. There was an ocean of deep love between them. It was the same with her Martha and Bradan. She'd experienced it many times.

"Why make them wait?" Mother said, clearly surprising them all.

"The marriage between Bradan and Martha is all right with me. It may eliminate eloping later."

"Alright," Da said. "I will marry you right away. But only if it is a Christian marriage in our church."

"And make it an outdoor wedding, weather permitting," Bradan added.

"Of course," Ken agreed.

"We wouldn't have it any other way," Bradan said.

The day of the double wedding dawned with bright, clear skies. A large, yellow sun blazed down on the lawn of Golden Ridge Baptist Church.

Mrs. Asquinn smiled with joy in the first row of chairs as she gazed upon her son. Both bridegrooms stood handsome looking in suit and ties in front of Pastor Asquinn. The best men also looked nice in their pressed tuxedos.

Pastor Asquinn walked down the aisle and greeted his daughter at the back of the church. As the organist played the opening strains of The Wedding March accompanied her, along with her wedding companions, down the aisle, along with Sherry and her father, and her wedding party.

The girls joined the boys at the front of the church. In the line the boys stood in the middle with Martha on Bradan's right side and Sherry on the outside on Ken's left side. When the girls had been handed over to their fiancés, Pastor Asquinn resumed his position as pastor. He began with Ken and Sherry first.

"Dearly beloved. We are gathered together this day, in the eyes of God, to join this man and this woman in holy matrimony. "God created this sacred union between man and woman to be a life-long commitment."

He paused and looked up at the guests. "If anyone here thinks these two should not marry for any reason speak now or forever hold their peace."

Martha looked sideways at Bradan. They exchanged glances, remembering Martin's earlier threat to maybe stop this union, but no one stirred to object. There was a collective letting out of the breath from the two couples as the Pastor continued. Bradan and Martha exchanged glowing smiles.

"Kenneth Murray Asquinn, do you take this woman to be your

lawfully wedded wife, through sickness or health, poverty or wealth, through the good as well as the bad, until death do you part?"

Ken gazed deep into Sherry's hazel eyes and smiled. "I do."

Pastor Asquinn turned his gaze upon Sherry. "Charlotte Julia Turehue, do you take this man to be your lawfully wedded husband through sickness or health, through poverty or wealth, through the easy times as well as hard times, till death do you part?"

Sherry gazed into Ken's deep blue eyes. "I do."

"And now I declare you man and wife," Pastor Asquinn declared. "You may kiss the bride."

Tenderly, Ken lifted and brought his lips down on hers.

When the two drew apart, Pastor Asquinn turned his attention to Martha and Bradan.

Martha's face glowed with the happiness within her as Da repeated the words. A thrill washed through Martha as she heard the words directed at her. She had sat through many ceremonies like this with her family, but there was no greater delight for her than to have the words directed at her and the man with whom she'd spend her life.

"Bradan Gerald Turehue, do you take this woman to be your lawfully wedded wife, through sickness or health, poverty or wealth, through the good as well as the bad, until death do you part?"

Bradan gazed deep into Martha's brown eyes and smiled. "Yes, sir, I do."

Pastor Asquinn turned his gaze upon Martha, "Martha Erma Asquinn, do you take this man to be your lawfully wedded husband through sickness or health, through poverty or wealth, through the easy times as well as hard times, till death do you part?"

Martha gazed into Bradan's deep brown eyes. "I do. I will be the best of helpmates to you."

"And now I pronounce you man and wife." Pastor Asquinn spoke the words clearly and proudly as he had with the first couple. "Bradan, you may kiss the bride."

Bradan folded his arms around Martha and she went to him willingly. Her lips sought his and when their lips met, she didn't want her husband to ever let her go. She was disappointed when their lips parted and Bradan released her. She was so weak from overwhelming love for her husband she almost fell and Bradan had to put her arms around her again so she'd stay on her feet.

Bradan and Martha then led the way between the double row of seats towards the house, through the necessary rain of rice, and the steps leading up to the front porch. Mother stopped at the bottom of the front steps as Martha paused, with Bradan beside her, on the top step; Ken and Sherry paused two steps below them. All four turned towards the waving well-wishers. Martha was the first to toss her bouquet which her baby sister, Faith, caught. When Sherry threw her bouquet, Audrey Baker, a classmate of the twins and Sherry from high school and Martha's maid-of-honour caught it.

"Let's hurry and change so that we can get going," Ken said.

The girls went to Martha's room to change into going-away clothes and the boys went to Ken's room. The four were reunited in the living-room.

"Ready to go at last," Ken said.

"I take it you aren't interested in any food before we go," Martha stated.

"No, I'm not," Ken assured them all. "I just want to get away. I feel like a caged bear about to be set free from confinement. Free!"

"I hear you," Bradan agreed.

The four retraced their steps through the front porch. Martha and Bradan led the way down the front steps to the patch of front lawn. Of course there were lots of cameras as family and friends wanted this event recorded as keepsakes.

At the cars, which were parked side by side in the family parking lot across from the front lawn, family hugged and parents said tearful good-byes.

"I didn't think I would be losing both my children to a wedding on the same day so soon," Mrs. Turehue sniffed. Mrs. Asquinn wiped tears from her eyes with a hankie.

Then it was Da's turn. Martha stood with Mother, Bradan, and Sherry as Da and son stood facing each other.

"Good-bye, Da," Ken said.

Martha felt relieved when Da placed an encouraging hand on his firstborn's shoulder and shook hands with the other.

"Good luck," he said in Welsh. "I do wish you the best in your chosen career."

"Thanks, Dad," Ken said. He released his father's hand and Da removed his other hand from Ken's shoulder.

"I wish you could have stayed in Ontario and been happy with our own provincial police force and not chosen to go thousands of miles away," he said sadly.

Martha cringed when Ken let out a disgusted sigh.

"Dad, we've been through this so many times I'm sick of it," Ken said.

"But, if you really believe this other force has more to offer, then so be it," Da finished.

"Dad, why did you think you had to leave Wales and all that was familiar to the family and come to Canada?"

The answer was complex and Martha felt that her brother knew the answer.

Da didn't answer. Instead, he said, "If you need anything, write, Ken. Even if it's money."

"I won't be needing that, Dad. I did put aside a substantial amount for this very occasion when Bradan and I worked on summer jobs."

"How about you, son?" Mr. Turehue inquired of Bradan. "How are you fixed for money?"

"I'm fine," Bradan assured his father.

Ken couldn't contain his impatience any longer. He opened his car door.

"May I help you inside, wife?" Ken said sweetly to Sherry.

"You may, husband."

He helped Sherry into the passenger seat and saw that she was settled before shutting the door and getting behind the wheel.

Martha worked free of the group, walked away and stopped in front of her twin, three younger brothers and younger sister, and Audrey. Audrey and Martin had been standing close together but quickly moved apart when Martha joined them. Martha and Martin watched as, with a wild yelp borne out of freedom, Ken drove across the lawn where the wedding had just taken place, through a gap in the trees and onto the road.

"Oh that man," Mam said, wiping a tear from a corner of her eye. "Dear God in heaven, please keep the four of them safe."

Da took her in his arms and offered her husbandly comfort. She rested her head on his shoulder and wept.

"Ken, my Ken, has flown from the nest. I'll pray every day that God will restore to him the joy of his salvation."

Martha looked gratefully at Martin and said, "I can't thank you enough for not preventing Bradan and I from getting married. You had the chance when Da asked if there was anyone who thought we shouldn't get married to speak up."

Martin shrugged and looked towards Audrey. "Oh, I don't know. Maybe Bradan's not so bad."

Martha followed his gaze and wondered if there was a romance blooming between Martin and Audrey.

She turned to her younger siblings. "Why are you guys looking so sad? Faith, you look about to cry."

"Ken's gone now," Faith said.

"So are you, Martha," Timmy said.

Martha wiped tears from the corner of his eyes with her hankie.

"Martin, you are the oldest of the family now," Ricky said.

"I guess I am. But only as long as Ken isn't around," Martin reminded them. "The worst we can do is throw up our hands in defeat and give up on them."

"Satan would love to see that," Martha agreed. "Don't give up on Ken or Bradan; pray for them constantly."

"We will," the younger children chorused.

"Martin, what will you do now?" Martha asked.

"I will continue schooling," Martin said. "I think it would be nice to teach school right here in Forest Lake; if not that, I want to be a high school teacher in Lakeview."

"Good for you, Martin," Martha said. "I hope you get the teaching position here in Forest Lake."

Bradan sauntered over.

"We will miss you on the school bus, Martha," Louise Fraser was saying.

"Who will occupy that third seat now?" Karen Aston said.

Bradan smiled. "If I remember the school bus, there will be plenty of kids to take her place. Everyone laughed over this.

"Let's get going, Mrs. Turehue."

A stream of teen-age friends and guests followed Bradan and Martha to his car. Some of the girls, even the boys, cried as Bradan opened the passenger side door and after helping Martha to be seated, closed the door. They waved as he backed out of the parking spot and drove down the hill and onto the road properly. Bradan drove in a more mannerly way than Ken had. He had just gained the road when Ken showed up behind him. Ken let out more whoops as he passed below the house that had been his home for so many years.

Martha saw Mother waiting with Martin and the younger children on the driveway close to the road for Ken to go by so they could wave to him. That they did and he and Sherry waved back. Martha and Bradan also waved good-bye to her siblings.

"I hope our Bradan fulfils at least one of those lofty dreams of his," Mrs. Turehue said. "My greatest concern is his salvation."

Da released his wife. His words were for Mr. Turehue and Mrs. Turehue as well as her.

"That boy is saved. His profession of faith as young a boy was genuine and Satan has merely turned him aside for a season. I was truly blessed to baptize Ken. Now this does not give him a license to sin. It should grief him greatly to sin. And as a true child of God the Holy Spirit will make his sins known to him and will cause him to seek mercy from his Lord for his sins. And He does show mercy on us, "for his mercy endureth for ever. He will be back. They both will."

Bradan took the direct route onto the road through Forest Lake. He drove until he reached the Arctic Watershed sign then pulled over and waited for his friend.

"Do we take different routes here," Martha said.

"Yep, we do," Bradan answered. "We go north and they go south. That's the way we decided it would be."

Shortly, Ken pulled up behind them and he and Sherry walked over to Bradan's car.

"We meet in Regina or near there to find accommodations," Ken said. "Am I right?"

"Not exactly," Bradan replied. Bradan knew their plans by heart. "I promised my cousin Garth we would show up at his place before Regina."

"Okay. Give me your cousin's address and we'll be there"

Bradan handed him a slip of paper, then Ken and Sherry went

back to Ken's car. As they parted company, Martha sat as close to her new husband as she could manage.

Bradan glanced at her. He had driven all the way from Forest Lake and would soon arrive in Thunder Bay. The eagerness to find a suitable motel and get her out of her travelling outfit and into bed, plain on his face. But, all he could do was gaze admiringly at her. Lovely. Impossibly beautiful. His.

Peering at him, Martha laughed out of sheer joy of anticipation.

He grinned at her and groaned. "I can't stand this. I'm not driving any further than the next motel."

At the next motel, Bradan parked and got out of the car. He came around to the passenger side and lifted Martha to the ground.

After registering, the couple paused outside the motel room while Bradan unlocked the door and swung it open. Without a word, he swept Martha up into his arms and stepped inside the motel room.

"Welcome home, Mrs. Turehue," he said.

Martha's eyes ran with tears. "I love you so much, Bradan Turehue."

Chapter Eleven
Cousin Garth

Bradan gripped the steering wheel and expertly steered the old car around a sharp curve in road. He was glad he gassed up the car before leaving Thunder Bay as the gas stations were far between and his car was a gas guzzler. The Trans-Canada Highway was narrow and winding here; rocky cliffs of the Canadian Shield towered above the road.

"I never thought I'd say this to my wife," Bradan said, "but, my precious one, please move closer to the passenger's side. I need room to steer."

Martha did as Bradan asked. She sat for the next few miles watching through the windshield as the last of Ontario's scenery passed by. She saw a sign.

"We've crossed the Manitoba-Ontario border," she said.

"Yes, we have," Bradan agreed.

The couple rode in silence as the scenery changed from towering rocks, trees, muskeg and lakes to fields of tall, maturing wheat for as far as the eye could see.

On Bradan drove, first driving through the huge city of Winnipeg, then beyond. At a gas station on the outskirts of a small town he stopped and gassed up the car again. When he crossed into Saskatchewan, he admitted to Martha he was a mite tired of driving and they should keep their eyes open for a motel for the night.

The next morning Bradan stopped his car where a smaller road joined the highway.

"Uh, oh."

"The road to your cousin Garth's is muddy and filled with ruts," Martha said.

"Looks like Garth was right about the rain when I talked to him on the telephone," Bradan said. "It's rained here for several days and this road shows it." Bradan cursed again.

"Bradan, darling, does it help the situation any taking God's name in vain like that?"

"Yes, it does." Bradan answered in a fashion Martha knew to be foreign to him. "It makes me feel better anyway."

He sat glaring at the rutted road, cursed again, and sighed deeply.

"Do you think Ken and Sherry are at your cousin's yet?" Martha asked.

"I wouldn't know," Bradan said. "They might be. I might as well get started."

He pressed on the gas and his car started on its journey through the quagmire.

"Now I will have to keep moving, no turning back," he said.

After a few minutes of watching her new husband fight the wheel to keep the vehicle on the road, Martha said. "I wish we had had the presence of mind to turn around and go back to town and find the where we spent the night and phone Garth from there. I'm sure he would have understood."

"I'm sure he would have," Bradan snapped.

The car bumped over a rough area, and she heard a scraping sound.

"There goes something on the undercarriage," Bradan said, and cursed again.

The road unfolded as straight as an arrow in front of them. The ditches were shallow but in places lined with sand hills and trees.

Martha suddenly sniffed. "What's that smell?"

Bradan sniffed. "Gas, that's what it is. Those stones back there must have punctured the tank. What foul, rotten disgusting luck."

"Will we have enough to get to Garth's farm?" Martha said.

Bradan shouted at her. "Don't ask so many silly questions. Of course we will!"

Offended, Martha moved to the edge of the seat closest to the window. "Sorry. I didn't want to do anything to rub you the wrong way."

Suddenly, the car began to slide, and there wasn't a thing Bradan could do to steer the vehicle and keep it on the road. The car ended up in the ditch, turned back onto the road, crossed it and hit the ditch on the other side, went back onto the road where it turned completely around and slid backwards for a way then went into the ditch again. The vehicle finally stopped, facing in the direction it had been going in the first place.

Bradan sat behind the wheel, helpless to do anything as the incident had shaken him considerably. He rested his head on his hands on the steering wheel. The incident had upset Martha, too.

Then, the engine sputtered and died.

"Oh damn. Now this car is out of gas."

"I'd best prepare myself to walk the rest of the way," Martha said. She opened her door and was about to step out but the ruts and mud stopped her.

Then two figures appeared by the car. Ken thumped lightly on Bradan's window to get his attention.

Bradan opened the window. "Hello, Ken, Sherry."

"Hello is right," Ken said.

The girls smiled and waved at each other.

"I saw that spin your car took," Ken said. "It surely was your guardian angel that kept the car from slamming into one of those sand hills. They may look innocent enough but there are huge rocks beneath the surface of the sand. Or you could have smashed into a tree and been killed."

Bradan answered, still visibly shaken. "I know, Ken. It's only by God's grace we weren't both killed."

Ken and Sherry helped Bradan and Martha out of the car.

Martha looked Ken over more thoroughly. There was a smile on her brother's face as she had never witnessed before. He looked sated. And Sherry – she positively glowed.

Martha and Sherry smiled at each other. They were glad to hear their husbands talk like this, giving God the credit for Bradan and Martha coming out of a very dangerous slide unscratched.

"How much farther is it to your cousin's house?" Ken said.

"Only another three miles," Bradan said. "We will need a ride. The gas leaked out when the tank was punctured."

"No problem at ol," Ken said in Welsh. "I'll help you transfer your stuff to my car."

After the luggage and Bradan's instruments were safe in Ken's car, Bradan said, "Now I need you to help me push this useless heap off the road. I'll steer while you push."

Once Bradan's car was off the road and not blocking the way for other traffic, the four reunited friends piled into Ken's car and got underway.

"How are you two doing back there?" Ken inquired after a mile or so. They had at last cleared the muddy part of the road. Now the road was gravelled and dusty.

"We are doing fine," Martha replied from among the luggage and instruments.

"I don't mind my wife sitting on my lap, at all," Bradan said. "Take it easy along here, Ken. We will be coming to Garth's driveway shortly."

Ken slowed.

"There it is, on the left," Bradan directed.

The road into Garth's yard was long, twisting and bumpy. At last some buildings, and then the house came into view.

"Park beside Garth's truck," Bradan said.

Bradan was out of the car as his cousin and his wife came out of the house to greet them. Martha joined him at his side.

"Hello, Garth, Peg."

"Bradan," Garth said, shaking hands with Bradan. "It's about time. We expected you hours ago."

"I kept having trouble with my stupid vehicle," Bradan said. "It's sitting in the ditch, crippled, not far from here. Garth, Peg, this is my wife, Martha.

"Wife?" Garth said surprised. He was taken aback at how young his cousin's wife was.

Ken and Sherry appeared by Bradan's side.

"And this is my good friend Ken Asquinn and his wife Sherry, my sister, whom you already know. Ken, Martha, my cousin Garth and his wife Peg."

Garth and Peg shook hands with Ken and Martha.

"Bradan's spoken a lot about you," Peg said to Ken. "And from what I see, what he said is true."

"Thank you. I guess," Ken said graciously.

"Come on in," Garth invited, "and join the party."

"You mean you started without us?" Bradan said. "I'll be along in a minute. Ken and I have to get something from the trunk."

Sherry followed Peg inside but Martha lingered.

Bradan accompanied Ken to the back of his car. He lifted the hood and Bradan grabbed a large jug of drink. Ken slammed the trunk lid shut and the friends went inside.

Garth looked at Bradan strangely. "When did you start drinking?"

Bradan shrugged.

"A while ago," Martha finally answered.

"Humph," Garth said. "I don't have a clue why you would start."

After that Bradan was swallowed up by family, and Ken quickly made friends that occupied his time, leaving the girls to fend for themselves. They knew what to expect from this night.

The girls were alone in some room in the house. From other parts of the house they could hear the party. It grew louder and louder.

"What time is it?" Martha said.

Sherry consulted a wall clock. "It's way past midnight."

Martha yawned. "I'm exhausted. And in your condition you should be in bed resting."

"So you noticed?"

"Sherry, you were glowing when we met out there on the road. Does Ken know yet?"

"Not yet. A doctor hasn't confirmed it. What about you? Anything like this happen to you and Bradan yet?"

"A doctor hasn't confirmed it. Just think, another generation of Turehueses."

"And Asquinns. Won't our mothers be overwhelmed when they hear the news?" Sherry said. "I am tired."

"I'm going to bed," Martha said.

"Where will we sleep?" Sherry wanted to know. "We weren't even assigned bedrooms."

Martha said. "Follow me."

She led the way outside, and to Ken's car.

"Perfect," Sherry said. "I'll sleep in the front while you curl up in the back the best you can. It's early enough in the season for the night to be warm yet."

The girls climbed into the car and pulled the doors shut behind.

Ken looked around the room in search of Bradan. He saw him leaning against the fireplace. He started for the door and signaled for Bradan to follow.

Ken stopped and waited beside some kind of storage shed close to the house, it was closer than any of the other buildings anyway. It happened to be the very building Ken had parked his car. The boys talking awakened Martha.

"Where are those wives of ours?" Ken said. "I haven't seen the girls anywhere. Have you?"

Bradan grunted. "They're likely hiding somewhere, afraid someone will take advantage of them. They would never let their hair down and enjoy themselves at a party like this."

Ken rebuked his friend. "And you ought to be glad about that. Sherry and Martha are both ladies. There are plenty of girls of questionable character here. Would you rather Martha be like one of them?"

Bradan didn't have to think very long about this. "You're right. I'll find Martha and leave with you."

Martha sat up and shook Sherry. "Wake up."

Martha opened the door got out of the car, followed by Sherry. Martha put one arm around Bradan's waist. "Here I am."

Sherry swept her arms around Ken's neck.

The boys, of course, were dumfounded to discover they had been so close all the time.

No one spoke for the longest of time.

"What's on your mind, Ken?" Martha finally asked.

"Bradan, what are we doing here?" Ken said.

Bradan answered immediately. "Having fun, I thought."

Ken challenged this. "Oh come on, admit it, my friend. You aren't having any more fun than I am."

"That's only your opinion," Bradan argued. "When he heard I was getting married, Garth invited us here to sort of bless our marriages."

Martha guffawed at this and reminded her husband, "Dad did that in Forest Lake during the ceremonies. I don't feel that this kind of shin ding is blessing anything. There's all kinds of evil deeds going on."

"I know," Bradan said. "Do you think we've sinned too much and lost any blessings God may have bestowed upon our marriages through Pastor Asquinn?"

"We likely will go too far if we hang around here," Martha said.

Bradan had had too much to drink and his mind was clouded.

"I'm not going anywhere. Garth invited me, and I intend to have fun," he said stubbornly.

"Suit yourself," Ken answered. "Sherry and I are leaving as quickly as we can."

"Are we leaving, dear?" Sherry said.

"Yes, we are leaving," Ken declared.

But before they could move, the house door burst open and partiers spilled outside, Garth among them.

"Bradan," he called. "Bradan where are you?"

Loud crashes and shouting spilled out from the walls of the house and into the dark night.

"I'd guess a fight has broken out," Martha said.

In action immediately, Ken said, "Get in the car."

An army of fun seekers advanced towards the foursome.

"I found you at last, Bradan," Garth crowed. "You aren't thinking of leaving so soon, are you? Running out on us?"

"No, I'm not running out on you," Bradan said. "I am simply thinking of my wife's reputation."

"And I'm thinking about my wife's reputation," Ken added.

But no one in the noisy mass listened.

"Ken," Garth was saying. "Isn't your Dad a Minister? I guess that's why you can't cut loose and enjoy yourself."

The rest laughed. One flapped his arms and made chicken noises.

This made Ken's blood boil. Sherry put a hand on his shoulder to calm him.

"Easy, Ken," Martha said. "Don't let these people get to you."

"Let's go, Ken, please," Sherry begged.

Ken brushed her hand away.

"I'll prove to these dorks nobody can drink me under the table," he said and started inside.

Bradan and Garth were alone with the girls.

Garth looked at Bradan and grinned sheepishly.

"Might as well come inside," he invited.

"Bradan," Martha said, but he brushed her plea aside and followed his cousin.

Chapter Twelve
Another Generation

Martha woke up in the back seat of the car the next morning well-rested about the same time as the party ended and everyone else exhausted. Sherry, who slept in front seat, also awoke and dressed for the day. Stiffly they opened the car doors and stepped outside, then went into the house and to the kitchen where they made themslves breakfast.

"I will wait until later on to brew up a fresh batch of coffee," Sherry said. "It won't be needed until later this afternoon."

After breakfast, in the living-room, Martha and Sherry stod side by side, surveying the mess the party had left behind.

The friends exchanged disgiusted glances.

"Might as well clean this up," Sherry said.

"But it isn't our duty to do so," Martha said, "But we may as well if we want the time to pass quickly."

"The only way for this to happen was to keep busy," Sherry said.

A couple of hours later, they went for a long walk. Martha marvelled at the expanse of the prairies, which she had not seen before.

Peg was in the kitchen when the girls returned to the farm house.

"We've already missed lunch and I'm starving," Sherry said

"Me, too," Martha said.

Peg wailed and placed a hand over her stomach.

"Oh, my."

"I'm sorry, I know we met last night, but I forget your name?" Martha said.

"I don't know if we did or not. I'm Peg. You are?"

"I'm Martha Asquinn—I mean Turehue. Bradan's wife."

"And I'm Sherry Asquinn. Ken's wife."

The older woman's eyebrows shot up in surprise. "Those two handsome hunks have wives?"

"They do," Martha said. "Us."

"They sure didn't act like it," Peg said in her scornful tone.

"Oh?" Sherry said.

"I don't believe what you are implying," Martha said. "Bradan would never do anything like that."

"Neither would Ken," Sherry said confident.

"I wouldn't mind having one of those handsome men for a husband," Peg stated without shame.

"Bradan will make a wonderful, outstanding husband and policeman, once he settles down." Martha defended her new husband.

Peg was skeptical. "And what makes you so sure? Why would those two be different? What are you two, anyway? I didn't see you swallow one drink last night."

"That's because we didn't," Martha said. "We are both Christians and believe in setting good examples and standing firm in our faith."

"We are all from Christian background. We all attend the same church," Sherry said.

"We did all attend the same church," Martha corrected her friend. "Remember Ken, and Bradan?"

Sherry said confidently. "They will settle down.

"Every day I pray to our God that Bradan will settle down and he the kind of husband I know and he knows he wants to be, and I know that eventually God will hear my prayers," Martha said.

Martha left the room and went in search of Bradan. She looked in a couple of the upstairs bedrooms before finding him. The drapes were drawn. It was dark and gloomy in the room so the first thing she did was open the curtains.

Then she went to the bed and shook Bradan gently.

"Bradan, darling. Don't you think it's time to wake up?"

Bradan opened his eyes, turned on his back and grimaced. He

quickly closed his eyes again.

"Martha, my love, what day is it?"

"It's way on into Sunday afternoon," Martha said.

Bradan didn't respond.

"Isn't it time to get up and be on our way to Regina?" Martha said. "It's almost four in the afternoon?"

"Wow, that late?" Bradan tried to sound as if he didn't know how late it was. He made no move to get up. Instead he turned on his side again and closed his eyes.

Thinking he was going back to sleep, Martha came closer to the bed.

When she came within his reach, Bradan reached out and pulled her onto the bed beside him.

"It is time I was stirring, Mrs. Turehue. But that can wait."

It was even later when Bradan eventually entered the kitchen with Martha behind him. Garth sat at the table, a steaming cup of coffee in front of him. A pot of freshly brewed brown liquid sat on the counter.

"Oh boy, coffee," Bradan said. Before Peg could move, Martha set a cup of coffee in front of him.

"Where were you two last night?" Garth asked the girls. "I didn't see anything of you after introductions."

"We behaved ourselves and stayed out of the way," Martha said.

"That's more than can be said about your husbands," Garth said. "Wow, the stuff you two drank and you claim to be Christians."

"Let's not talk about that, okay?" Martha pleaded, seeing the annoyed look on Bradan's face.

"Okay, okay. Where did you say you ditched your car, Bradan?"

"Alongside the road after the slippery muddy section. The gas tank was punctured at some point along the way."

Garth whistled. "That will cost a lot to get repaired."

"And to refill the tank with gas," Bradan said. "I don't have that kind of money to spend on that heap."

"What will you do?" Garth said. "Did you want to leave the car here and work on it another time, or maybe sell it?"

"I'd rather sell it," Bradan said. "I don't have any money, not even for living quarters once we hit Regina."

"I'll take that heap off your hands," Garth said and named a price.

"Fair enough," Bradan said. "Before I finalize anything I will have to talk to Ken about me and my wife traveling with him and Sherry."

"I understand," Garth said.

"By the way, has anyone seen Ken yet today?" Bradan inquired.

"No," said Martha.

"I've been wondering where he is," Sherry said. "We didn't sleep in the house so we have no idea where he got to."

"He didn't come inside to sleep," Bradan said.

"I'll find him," Peg said.

Sherry intervened. "Oh, no you won't. I will."

"You might find him," Peg agreed with a twist of her painted voluptuous lips. "But I'll tell you what. He won't remember that he's married."

Sherry glared at her, refusing to believe what Peg was implying.

She looked straight at Peg and said. "I will find him and he will remember me."

"I'll kelp you," Martha said.

Bradan was on his feet in a flash. "And I'll help you help her search."

Martha was the first one out the door with Bradan and Sherry following close behind her.

As Martha had already noticed about the prairies, the wind blew relentlessly and continuously, as it did now. It whipped her hair around her head, her face, eyes and mouth. She had to lean against the wind in order to keep her balance. But the sky was clear and the sun hot, hotter than she ever remembered it in Forest Lake.

"The first place to look would be his car," Bradan said.

"Ken," Sherry called softly as she approached. There was no movement inside. She peeked in through the windows but saw no one. She called louder.

"Ken."

No answer.

"Ken!" she shouted.

The searchers passed the last of the buildings; on the edge of his property grew a belt of trees. Grass grew tall here. There were also hay bales piled by the trees.

Martha caught sight of something lying on one of these bales.

She waved to catch the attention of Bradan and Sherry.

"Over here."

Martha pointed and Sherry approached carefully.

"Let's take a closer look," Sherry suggested and called softly, "Ken."

Martha was relieved when her brother stirred and sat up.

"Yes, Charlotte, my love."

When Sherry reached out a hand towards him, Ken grasped her wrist and pulled her down beside him.

"Mrs. Asquinn," he said with adoration. "It's time you got here."

"Have you been out here all day by yourself?" Martha said.

"I guess I have," Ken said. "I stayed out here because it's peaceful."

"I had my fill of noise and foolishness last night, too," Bradan said.

Martha touched Bradan's elbow and signaled that perhaps they should go and leave the two alone.

Later, Ken and Sherry arrived back at the house.

"Coffee," Ken said to Sherry the instant he saw his pal at the table with a full cup in front of him. Garth was nowhere in sight.

Martha wondered how things stood between Garth and Peg. Garth could not bear being in the same room as his wife for long.

"I'll get you some," Peg said.

But Sherry already held the coffee pot in one hand and a cup in the other. She set the cup in front of Ken and poured. He swallowed, and a look of pure delight lit up his face.

"This is delicious."

While Sherry returned the coffee pot to its stand on the counter, Peg took this opportunity to sit in the chair next to Ken, making certain she was as close to him as possible.

This maneuver did not faze Sherry at all. She moved another chair and sat down between her and Ken. Peg had no choice but to move. She walked to the sink in a huff and stood there glowering back at everyone in the room.

Sherry smiled sweetly at Ken when he glanced her way.

"More coffee, please," Bradan requested politely.

"Me too," Ken said.

Martha looked Peg's way.

"You are standing right next to the coffee pot," she told her.

"So you can serve these men more coffee," Sherry said, adding to the woman's humiliation.

Peg did so in a huff. This done she went to the telephone on the wall.

"I wonder who she's phoning?" Sherry said.

"I'd guess a taxi," Martha said.

Peg stood with her back towards the table. She was not the only one in the room relieved when a taxi finally pulled into the yard. She collected her purse and was ready to leave.

"Bye," Sherry said sweetly.

"I could see sparks flying between you three women," Ken said. "I want to know what's going on."

"Oh, Peggy tried to convince Martha and me we are too immature and inexperienced to hang onto our men," Sherry said. "She tried driving a wedge between you and me, and Bradan and Martha."

"Furthermore, she tried to convince both of us it wouldn't be us, but her, you two left for Regina with," Martha said.

"How stupid!" Bradan said. He put an arm around Martha's waist. "Why would I want to leave with anyone but you? No one is going to drive a wedge between us. I love you."

"I know, Bradan. And I love you."

"I know who I will be leaving with," Ken said. He drew Sherry towards him. "My lovely little wife, Sherry."

Garth had come back into the room and sat down without one question about his wife and had taken this all in without a word. Now, he looked at each of the foursome with respect.

"If there's such a thing as true love in this world, then you four certainly have it," he said.

"Ken we have some business to discuss," Bradan said.

"What business is that?"

"Travel arrangements. You know my car is nonoperational and I don't have the money to repair it. I used up the last of the money buying refreshments for the party last night."

Martha glanced at him, her eyebrows raised in surprise. She knew, and so did Sherry, and Ken, that Bradan had lots of money in the bank. The trust fund his father had set up for him when he sold the house her family now lived in, lay relatively untouched in a bank back in Lakeview. But apparently he didn't want just anyone to know about this money, and she respected his wishes so kept quiet.

"And?" Ken prompted when his friend paused.

"I was wondering if Martha and I could travel with you and Sherry."

"Absolutely. I would hate to see my best friend, and his wife, walking."

"Thanks, pal," Bradan said.

Car doors opened and closed and then a car drove away.

"That will be Peg returning home with the children," Garth said.

Four pairs of eyes started blankly at him.

"But she left here in a taxi a short while ago," Martha said.

"She went into town for the children," Garth explained. "We left them with their grandparents overnight."

"Oh," Martha said.

"That makes sense," Sherry said.

Soon two girls and a boy noisily burst through the door into the kitchen. They went to Bradan and Sherry for hugs and greetings, and then were introduced to Ken and Martha.

"It's Uncle Ken, and Aunt Martha. We're all family now," Garth informed the children

"Will you play for us?" the oldest of the three inquired.

"You mean me alone?" Ken asked.

"No, both of you."

"Sure," Ken answered. Martha knew Bradan expected him to.

Instruments were brought in from the car.

"Bradan," Martha began, "seeing that this is Sunday, I was wondering about church this evening."

Bradan let out a loud groan. "Oh, no!"

"And don't bother me about church, either," Ken commanded Sherry.

Martha pleaded some more. "But we thought if we went into town on our own we wouldn't have to bother you two."

"I said don't bother me," Bradan said.

Ken said promptly. "No. Sherry, you are not taking the car out over that muddy road. You are not experienced driving in mud."

"I am. I can drive them into town," Peg said.

Ken and Bradan exchanged looks.

"All right," Ken consented, and handed Peg the car keys

"But don't linger after church," Bradan instructed Martha.

"We won't," Martha said.

Martha and Sherry used the bathroom to freshen up in, and were soon ready to leave for church.

"The boys are already outside coaxing music from those strings," Sherry said.

The boys continued to play. Sherry loved Ken's energetic moving of the bow, hearing music flow forth in great splendour.

A wave of homesickness swept over Martha. She thought of peaceful Sunday evenings at home, attending church with family. Why was her new husband here playing tunes that offered no spiritual value?

"Don't you feel guilty for not going to church with your wife, or at least driving her and the girls into town so we could attend?" Sherry asked the question before Martha formed the words.

"Why aren't you in church instead of here recovering from a senseless, excessive hangover?" Martha said.

The music never faltered.

With a shrug of her shoulder, Martha brushed these intrusive thoughts away and continued listening to tunes about all kinds of human depravity; but thoughts of peaceful Sundays and more important, peace of mind, would not leave her. She couldn't help wonder if their husbands played more energetically to try and shake off the feelings of quilt and quench the Holy Spirit. But the Holy Spirit would not leave her alone. She glanced at the audience. Three young faces, along with their dad, gazed with wonders at the players. She lifted the youngest, a girl about four years old, onto her lap and held her close.

"These are your nieces and nephews, darling," Martha told Bradan, a sad look on her face. "You should be singing better-quality songs, setting a finer example."

Suddenly, Bradan stopped playing. An unrecognizable sound like music came from Ken's fiddle and he gawked at Bradan. Bradan's brown eyes shooting darts of fire at his wife.

"And what kind is that?"

"The kind I had while growing up," Martha answered.

Ken turned his head away from his friend and snickered. Ken laughed a short, mean laugh and stood up. With his head turned away from his wife, Bradan returned his instruments to their cases and put them in the vehicle.

"I don't know why you think they should hear that kind of music," he retorted and stalked away.

Sherry touched her friend's shoulder with a hand. "We'd better get going or we'll be late for the church service."

Three months later.....

It was a glorious September morning in Regina with a blue, cloudless sky. The two couples had parted company with Garth and his family, over two months ago and were settled in a nice apartment close to where the boys trained.

Ken and Bradan sat in lavender-coloured cushioned chairs in a downtown doctor's waiting room. Martha was called into the doctor's. When she emerged, Sherry was called in.

Silently, and smiling happily, Martha sat down in a seat next to Bradan. She whispered into his ear and a look of sheer wonderment passed over his handsome face. He stood up and gathered Martha in his arms and kissed her.

"You're sure?"

Martha nodded, beaming. "We are about to start another generation of Turehueses."

When Sherry emerged from the doctor's office, she joined Ken. There was a certain secret smile tugging at the corners of her mouth. She lowered her head closer to Ken's ear and said something to him.

He gathered her in his arms and kissed her.

"A new generation of Asquinns, you and me," he said, dazed, as if he couldn't register all that he'd heard.

Sherry kissed him.

His arms around Sherry, Ken turned to Bradan and Martha and said, "What a blessed event. A baby! We are truly blessed of the Lord!"

Bradan grabbed Sherry and lifting her off her, feet, twirled her around and around. "Children are a wonderful heritage of the Lord."

In the car, driving back to their apartment, Sherry sat in the front seat with her husband while Martha and Bradan occupied the backseat. In spite of the feeling of doubt and grief plaguing her over the last few years, she felt God's presence and a promising future with Bradan. With her hope fixed on heaven, Martha breathed a prayer.

Over a thousand kilometers away, across two provinces, a family also said a prayer. Martin knelt by his easy chair, and Da, Mam and the younger children knelt by their seats, too.
"Father, I leave Ken in your hands," Martin prayed. "The future of his, and Bradan's family, too, is in your charge. Amen."
"Amen," Da echoed.
"Amen," Mam and the children all said as one.

Martha opened her eyes and suddenly a peaceful sensation filled her from the top of her head to the tip of her toes. She knew folks back home were praying for her, Sherry, Ken and Bradan. She smiled at Sherry. She knew the future might be rough at times, but in general it would be a good life. She ran her fingers over her tummy. A future that included this child. Bradan's child. And God.

TO BE CONTINUED.........what are the girls, and their children, to expect from the future with their backslidden husbands? Who is the mysterious person that's watched Ken and Braden from boyhood and what happens to him?

Find out whether the ending will make you weep or cheer or both, by reading Book Three, The Asquinn Twins: No Greener pastures.

Other Books By Grace Brooks
The Asquinn Twins Series

The Asquinn twins Come to Forest Lake. Book One
Where The Trail Forks: Book Two
No greener Pastures: Book Three.
Sihon. Book Four.

Books Five Six and Seven are works in progress.

A Dog For Keeps under the pen name Lynette Tamar Mark (audio book) Snow Queen's Forever Home: Iinda Grace Brooks

GRACE BROOKS

The Asquinn Twins Book 2: Where The Trail Forks

www.ingramcontent.com/pod-product-compliance
Lightning Source LLC
Chambersburg PA
CBHW071526080526
44588CB00011B/1567